Minnesota Grit

Minnesota Grit

The Men Who Defeated the James-Younger Gang

By
John Koblas

NORTH STAR PRESS OF ST. CLOUD, INC.

For Renegade & Cowgirl—
Some Cowboy Honor

Cover art: Hans Werner

Copyright © 2005 John Koblas

ISBN: 0-87839-215-7

First Edition
April 2005

All rights reserved. No part of this book may be reproduced in any form without the written permission of the publisher.

Printed in the United States of America by Versa Press, Inc., East Peoria, Illinois.

Published by:
North Star Press of St. Cloud, Inc.
P.O. Box 451
St. Cloud, Minnesota 56302
nspress@cloudnet.com

Contents

J.S. Allen 1
Adelbert Ames 2
George Bradford 16
John Bresett 18
Alonzo E. Bunker 21
Sherman E. Finch 25
Sheriff James Glispin 29
Joseph Lee Heywood 32
Reverend Francis Howard 39
Michael Hoy 41
Anselm R. Manning 49
William Wallace Murphy 53
Charles A. Pomeroy 59
General Edmund Mann Pope 60
Benjamin A. Rice 70
S.J. "Slim" Severson 71
Asle Oscar Sorbel 71
Elias Stacy 78
Thomas Lent Vought 78
Dr. Henry Mason Wheeler 81
Frank J. Wilcox 89
Notes 93

NORTH STAR DEFENDERS
(Dedicated to the Minnesota heroes of 1876)

That thunder isn't thunder that we hear:
It's horses' hooves and gunshots in the street,
So grab your guns, defend our Northfield town
And rout the bloody outlaws in defeat.

They're heading down the Cannon River now.
They're desperate men, hard-footin' men, and hurt.
Behind us, honest citizens lie dead.
We'll chase them till we serve their just dessert.

The thunder of their hooves is weakening:
They're split up near the Minneopa Falls.
They carry bullets from our Northfield guns.
One group is riding but another crawls.

Though weeks have passed, we're Minnesota grit.
A battle of our guns at Hanska Slough
Subdues the outlaws—one subdued to death.
Their murdering and thieving days are through.

—Roger Brezina

To Sharon and Frank
Best Wishes always,
Roger Brezina
9-29-05

Introduction

THEY CAME FROM ALL WALKS of life and from communities all over south central Minnesota—Northfield, Madelia, Mankato, Minneapolis, St. Paul. These were the "helpless" citizens of Minnesota whom outlaw Bill Stiles told Jesse James "wouldn't know a band of outlaws if they surrounded them." But when the notorious James-Younger Gang rode into Northfield on September 7, 1876, they found out that "taking candy from a baby" was anything but easy.

During the bungled robbery attempt, outlaws Clell Miller and Bill Stiles (A.K.A. Bill Chadwell) lay dead in the streets of Northfield at the hands of sharpshooters Henry M. Wheeler and Anselm R. Manning, while their retreating companions, literally shot to pieces, could barely stay in their saddles. Posses from all over Minnesota, led by such daring figures as Mike Hoy, John Bresett, Edmund Pope, Sherman E. Finch, and W.W. Murphy pursued them for two weeks in penetrating rain, culminating in a shootout in Hanska Slough near La Salle. Outlaw Charlie Pitts was shot and killed by these gallant citizens, and the three Youngers so badly wounded, they had no choice but to surrender. Only Frank and Jesse James escaped, but like the Youngers, their bodies had been riddled with bullets.

MINNESOTA GRIT

This book is not about the exploits of the James-Younger Gang; it is, instead, a tribute to the heroes who defeated the gang in Minnesota and deserve the real recognition they seldom receive. While there were hundreds of brave men who stood up to the outlaws, few of their names were recorded to be mentioned in the pages of this tribute. Listed here, however, are those heroes who deserve particular attention—a handful of special men, who risked life and limb to answer the call. All of these men displayed true Minnesota Grit:

The seven captors of the Younger brothers on the steps of the Flander's Hotel, Madelia, in 1876. Left to right: Sheriff James Glispin, Captain W.W. Murphy, G.A. Bradford, B.M. Rice, Colonel T.L. Vought, C.A. Pomeroy, and S.J. Severson. (Courtesy of the Northfield Historical Society)

J.S. Allen

J. S. ALLEN AND TWO OTHER NORTHFIELD citizens were standing on the corner talking on September 7, 1876, when eight suspicious looking men rode into town in three groups. Francis Howard was the first citizen to notice them, and he immediately became suspicious and followed them.

Howard quickly approached Allen and his companions and shared his fears with them. Allen quickly left the men on the Northfield street corner, walked to the bank door and attempted to look in. Immediately, Clell Miller stepped out of the doorway and grasped Allen by the lapel of his coat. Miller quickly drew his revolver and, in swinging it over his head, began shooting a volley of shots into the air and shouting, "Get out of there, you sons of bitches."

According to Allen, who later recounted his part in the chaos: "I have lived in Northfield since 1856. I am engaged [in] business here. I saw three men coming over [the] bridge on horseback. I says, 'Who are those men? I don't like the looks of them.' About [the] same time there were two others [who] came across [the] bridge. I came to Scriver's corner, saw three sitting on [a] dry goods box. I said to Ino Acker, 'I believe they are here to rob the bank.' Then the three that were there went and met the two others standing about [the] bank. The first three went into [the] bank. I started for [the] bank [and] as I got [to] the bank door, [I] saw Mr. Heywood. The man inside came to [the] door, took me by [the] collar and says, 'You son of a bitch, don't you holler.' I broke [into] a run. Then they began shooting. I know none of the men."[1]

As Allen jerked free from Miller, he raced towards a store around the corner shouting, "Get your guns, boys. They are robbing the bank." Citizen H.B. Gress saw Allen break free and knew immediately what was transpiring. "Up to that time I had no idea what was to occur," said Gress. "I hollered at once, 'They are robbing the bank.' And it was taken up from store to store until the whole business part of the town was aroused to the situation."[2]

After rushing into the hardware store of Anselm R. Manning to spread word of the robbery in progress, Allen re-entered his own store and shouted the news to his clerks.

In November 1889, J.S. Allen sold his store to the partnership of Allan & Phillips and left Northfield.[3]

Adelbert Ames

MEDAL OF HONOR RECIPIENT ADELBERT AMES lived nearly a century. Born at Rockland, Maine, October 31, 1835, he was the son of Captain Jesse and Martha Bradbury Tolman Ames. His father, Captain Ames had been born at Vinal Haven, Knox County, Maine, on February 4, 1808. Jesse Ames left the farm and went to sea when he was but fifteen years old. By the time he was twenty-three, he assumed command of a merchant vessel.[4]

Adelbert's mother, Martha, the daughter of Thomas Tolman of Rockland, Maine, married Captain Ames on October 27, 1832, and twice sailed around the world with her husband. Jesse made his last voyage in 1861 after thirty years at sea as a captain, stopped in New Zealand, went on to London and finally settled in Minnesota that same year.

Because his father was a master mariner, Adelbert served as a sailor and later as mate on a clipper ship.[5] In 1856, at the age of twenty, he was appointed to the United States Military Academy at West Point and graduated fifth in his class in May 1861. He was commissioned a lieutenant of artillery. Within a month of his commission, Ames launched a brilliant military career while serving in the Civil War.

Ames commanded a section of Battery D, Fifth U.S. Artillery, at the First Battle of Bull Run and was seriously wounded in the thigh. He issued orders until he was unable to continue, refusing to leave the field. Brevetted a major for his courage, he returned to duty in a few weeks. Ames commanded Battery A, Fifth U.S. Artillery, in the Peninsula Campaign, led the Twentieth Maine Infantry in the Antietam Campaign and at Fredericksburg, Virginia, and was present at the siege of Yorktown, and the battles of Gaines's Mills and Malvern Hill, besides many of the minor engagements in Virginia throughout the Civil War. He was brevetted colonel for gallantry and commanded a brigade and at times a division in the army of the Potomac, as well as in the operation before Petersburg fell in 1864. He was brevetted major-general of volunteers for his conduct at the capture of Fort Fisher, 13 March 1865, and brevetted major-general, United States army, for "gallant and meritorious conduct in the field during the rebellion." He served as Major General George G. Meade's aide at the Battle of Chancellorsville. In 1863, Ames was commissioned a brigadier general of volunteers, and he commanded a division at the battles of Gettysburg, Cold Harbor, Petersburg, and Fort Fisher. Ames was brevetted major general of volunteers and major general in the Regular Army for his efforts.[6]

In distinguishing himself at Bull Run and Gettysburg, he earned a Medal of Honor. He was later promoted to brigadier general in the Eleventh Corps of the Army of the Potomac before taking command of a division in Major General Benjamin F. Butler's Army of the James in Virginia.[7]

General Ames was mustered out of the volunteer service in April 1866, one of the last volunteer officers to be discharged. Prior to his discharge, he wrote to his mother that he was tired of "Rebel Watching." Ames was of the opinion that, "Fire still burns in the hearts of the people here, and our star-spangled banner or our country's uniform are only needed to fan the flame into wrath."[8]

While serving as federal post commander in Columbia, South Carolina, Ames quickly set himself at odds with the people of the state. About 7,500 Union troops were posted in South Carolina. A drunken white trooper accosted two citizens when they refused to listen to his bullying comments. The soldier wrestled one of the men to the ground, drew his pistol, and fired a shot that just missed his victim's ear. A former Confederate soldier drew a pistol and killed the Union cavalryman.[9]

The dead soldier's compatriots threatened vengeance on the townsfolk. A former Southern officer blocked them, warning the Union sergeant: "If you do not [stop these] threats and march your company back to their quarters, [you] must take the consequences. There are . . . six hundred ex-Confederates [here] who might no longer be restrained."[10]

Adelbert Ames, however, felt the former Confederates should be punished. He ordered his troops to arrest both the killer and the abused citizen. Because both men had already left town, Ames instead arrested former Confederate General Martin Gray and several others, charging them with "complicity." The men were jailed with common criminals, much to the ire of the citizens.

Upon his discharge, Ames was appointed a lieutenant colonel in the Twenty-fourth U.S. Infantry, but he took a leave of absence and went to Europe. While he was on the continent, Congress decided to reconstruct the former Confederate states. Ames joined his regiment in Mississippi in August 1867 and was appointed military governor of Mississippi in June 1868. A few months later, Adelbert Ames was put in charge of the Fourth Military District, which included not only Mississippi, but Arkansas as well.[11]

The Mississippi Legislature chose Ames for the United States Senate in 1869. He was immediately looked upon as an example of a corrupt reconstruction politician in the South, but it is doubtful he was the rogue pictured by some historians. Instead, "he was probably an honest man caught in events quite beyond his control."[12]

Provisional governor of Mississippi via an appointment from President U.S. Grant, the "carpetbag" senator married Butler's daughter Blanche during the summer of 1870. The Senate finally agreed that, although it was unorthodox, Ames could serve as both provisional governor and in the Senate simultaneously. Ames's objective, while in office, was to enforce the Fourteenth Amendment to the Constitution. While promoting civil rights, Ames "authorized all persons, without respect to race, color, or previous condition of servitude, who possesses the qualifications prescribed by the laws . . . to act as jurors."[13]

His term in the Senate began pretty much in a routine way, but, following a clash with Senator Frank Blair of Missouri during a debate over the Fourteenth Amendment, Ames made some political enemies in the South, including the president of the Senate. Ames was adamant that Blair was not doing all he could to help the black freemen and former slaves and wrote: "[Blair] certainly does not soar very high in his flights, hardly beyond the fumes of the barroom."[14]

In September 1870, Blanche Ames, wife of Adelbert, wrote her mother in one of her letters from Northfield: "It is not regular prairie here, but all hills and vales—and the grass is beautiful; all through the town it is close white clover turf, but on the unplowed lands the goldenrod, fringed gentian, and a thousand flowers are in bloom."[15]

Blanche also informed her mother about their beautiful, spacious estate on South Division Street: "The house is very neatly and comfortably furnished, perfectly new—rooms spacious, walls smooth finish, pleasant bay windows in dining room, and sitting room. The house is the center of a square filled with trees and a vegetable garden. My chamber and dressing room are in front of the house over the parlor and entry. The windows look over the field to the (Cannon) river and woods beyond."[16]

The lavish Ames mansion, which housed Jesse and his wife, as well as Adelbert and his wife, was constructed from plans that had originally appeared in *Harpers Magazine*. As early as 1866, Adelbert had written his parents about plans as being suitable for their new home, and he had offered to help furnish the house. The home became the showplace of the town, and local citizens always turned their heads at his magnificent team and carriage.

Blanche wrote: "Apples, pears, peaches they [Adelbert's parents] buy, but there are melons of all kinds, and plums by the quantity in the garden. The market is good—prairie chicken, pigeons, and venison make a pleasing variety. Mrs. Ames has [seventy-two] chickens, two cows, and lots of bees. I have a large piece of honey and delicious graham muffins from fresh meal ground at the mill, every night. The table is well set, with silver and white damask, plates are changed, courses changed as well as they are at home."[17]

Troubled with Southern politics, Adelbert's heart was home in Northfield where he shared the mansion with his parents and then his wife. "Father has completed his barn, which I honestly believe is better, so far as relates to the strength, material, workmanship, etc., than any house in town, his own excepted," wrote Ames to his wife on June 20, 1871. "It is surmounted by a cupola like the tower on yours, with a horse for a vane. The whole structure [is] complete in all of its parts. Business with our mill is and has been good. The crop will probably be an average one. Thus the prospect for next year seems a good one."[18]

Ames wrote Blanche again on July 26, 1871, hopeful that events in Mississippi would take a turn for the better: "I have letters from my friends in Miss[issippi] urging me to be there in Sept[ember] as they will then have a state convention—when a 'new departure' may be taken—at least I hope so, so far as the Gov[ernor] is concerned. I must try to be there and ventilate my notions on the situation. No hog on ice was ever more independent than I am, and shall be in matters political. Shall I make a speech I have no doubt I shall show it, not rudely or coarsely, but clearly and unmistakably."[19]

In 1874, he was elected governor of Mississippi with a black running mate, A.K. Davis, as lieutenant governor. Ames had hoped to remake Mississippi into the model of New England. Ames despised the South, writing to his wife that "slavery blighted this people." Ames, however, held his fellow carpetbaggers in no better regard, calling them "an audacious, pushing crowd," who were out to loot the state. He grew disillusioned by the ignorance and corruption of the blacks he worked with as well. His connection with Beast Butler, and his own high-strung personality, made him anything but popular with Southerners.[20]

Ames, however, had the misfortune of becoming governor at the time when Southern whites were reestablishing their power. He refused to bend to their wishes as evidenced by his Inaugural Address of 1874:

"[He] made an earnest plea for kindly feelings between the whites and the blacks, politically, saying that they are now in all other things as closely united as are people of the same surroundings elsewhere. He advocated early preparation for educating the ignorant, advised that more attention be paid to manufacturing, and strongly urged that more breadstuffs be raised. To this end he recommended that the large plantations be cut up into small farms and sold to the men who till them."[21]

In March, he declared that he was determined to be, "Governor of the whole people, dealing out impartial justice to all." Southern whites were infuriated, and the Ku Klux Klan formed "white guards" who were stationed at polling places. Ames appealed to President Grant for federal troops but was turned down.[22]

Under the leadership of Senator Lucius Q.C. Lamar, Mississippi whites devised a scheme to retrieve their state from "carpetbag-scalawag black rule." The group nominated white Democrats for every office and implemented measures to make certain they succeeded. "It was not a campaign, it was a revolution!" Ames was helpless![23]

On August 5, 1874, he wrote to Blanche: "The election at Vicksburg passed off quietly only because the Democrats, or white man's party, had both intimidated the blacks and perpetrated frauds of registration, which made their success a certainty, so, of course, they had no cause to commit murder. Had there been a doubt as to the issue, a bloody riot would have resulted."[24]

One week later, Ames wrote to Blanche: "Mississippi, which has commanded my thoughts and time for the last six years, has lost its power over me for forever. And I profit by experience I hope. I have enough honors for a long while, and as I look to a quiet home life as the most certain source of true happiness, I have no cause to grieve over any fate, however adverse, to my political preferment this state may have in store for me. We can say quits at any time, and she will be my debtor."[25]

As rumors of impeachment began to sweep over him, his position became increasingly difficult. Although he wished to retire and go home to Northfield, he felt he could not do so with charges hanging over him. He knew there was no just cause of impeachment to be found, but he also knew the ruthless character of his opponents.[26]

Ames's excursion into Southern politics ended quite abruptly. After only a little over a year in office, he faced impeachment by a hostile Mississippi Democratic legislature, which had been elected in 1875 via what some described as "fraud, intimidation, and violence." On February 25, 1876, the Mississippi House of Representatives passed a resolution by a vote of 86 to 14, impeaching him for "high crimes and misdemeanors in office." Lieutenant-Governor Davis was also to be tried.[27]

Adelbert Ames was charged with inciting the Vicksburg riots, marching the black militia, appointing incompetents to positions for corrupt motives, and granting unnecessary prison pardons. He was initially charged with eleven infractions during the impeachment proceedings, but in the weeks to come, the number of grievances grew considerably.

General Benjamin Butler came to his son-in-law's defense, although the Mississippi Legislature had by then gained the zenith of its power. Butler wrote to Ames on February 25, 1876, from Washington: "I have got into communication with Lamar through Judge Black and Beck, and Lamar has undertaken to stop the procedure as well as he can. I have seen Black, and I may send him down as counsel when the trial comes on, which may not be for a week. Lamar thinks that Wathall will be good counsel, and is against impeachment, and has gone or is going from Lamar to try to stop it."[28]

On March 21, 1876, Blanche Ames wrote her mother from Jackson, Mississippi: "Mr. Durant replies to the impeachment charges tomorrow, and the trial begins a week from tomorrow. There is but little suspense, as we can anticipate but one result—conviction."[29]

Although Congress cleared him of all charges, he resigned on March 28, 1876, and his political career in the South was finished. His letter of resignation read: "Gentlemen: In reply to your suggestion, I beg to say that in consequence of the election last November, I found myself confronted with a hostile Legislature, and embarrassed and baffled in my endeavors to carry out my plans for the welfare of the State, and of my party.

"I had resolved, therefore, to resign my office as governor of the State of Mississippi; but meanwhile proceedings of Impeachment were instituted against me, and of course, I could not, and would not retire from my position under the imputation of any charge affecting my honor or integrity.

"For the reasons indicated, I still desire to escape burdens which are compensated by no possibility of public usefulness; and if the Articles of Impeachment presented against me were not pending, and the proceedings were dismissed, I should feel at liberty to carry out my desire, and purpose of resignation."[30]

On presentation of this letter to the Mississippi House of Representatives, a resolution was passed dismissing the Articles of Impeachment by formal procedure. On March 29, 1876, the Mississippi Senate passed a similar resolution. Ames' final message to the people of Mississippi was: "I hereby respectfully resign my office as Governor of Mississippi."[31]

Ames told a reporter from a New York newspaper, "It is not safe for any Northern man . . . to live there, if his convictions incline him to the cause of humanity and if he attempts any accurate measures, especially political efforts in behalf of the colored people of the state."[32]

Describing the proceedings in a letter to General Butler, Ames' attorney wrote: "This plan was carried out without any reflection on the governor's character. Indeed, he stands better today in the estimation of his enemies as ever before. Throughout the trying crises he bore himself as a brave and honorable gentleman."[33]

Ames had previously raised $40,000 from friends in the East, and upon arriving in Minnesota he purchased part of the Northfield Mills from his father, Jesse, the former sea captain from Maine. Returning to Northfield in 1876, he wrote, "Thus our new life begins. But I have not grown to a business frame of mind—an occupation."[34]

The mill in Northfield had been in the Ames family since October 1864 when Adelbert's father, Jesse, often addressed as "Captain" because he had sailed the seas for thirty years, made twenty to thirty voyages to Europe, repeatedly visited South America, and twice sailed around the world, purchased the mill from Charles A. Wheaton. Jesse Ames had arrived in Northfield in 1861 to visit a son and liked the state so well, he remained. The firm of Jesse Ames & Sons consisted of a mill on the east side of the Cannon River and an old saw mill on the west bank. In 1869, they built a new and larger mill on the site, employed twenty-five men, and turned out 175 barrels of flour daily. Jesse Ames's mill was one of the first to turn out the new process patent flour, which won the prize at the Philadelphia Exposition.[35]

When Cole Younger appealed for a pardon in 1897, he wrote: "We had been informed that ex-Governor Ames of Mississippi and General Benjamin Butler of Massachusetts had deposited $75,000 in the National of that place, and it was the above information that caused us to select the bank of Northfield."[36]

A few years later, Cole told State Parole Agent F.A. Whittier that the reason Northfield was chosen was that the gang "hoped to meet Butler on one of his visits to Minnesota, and if not [they] were to get even with him in a measure by raiding this bank, which [they] did."[37]

Younger became obsessed with the idea of getting back the money he felt Butler and Ames had stolen from the South. Cole Younger later wrote, "As had J. T. Ames, Butler's son-in-law . . . we felt little compunction, under the circumstances, about raiding him or his [bank]."[38]

He told the interviewer in 1915 that he had thought of his friends, the James boys, who like him, were fugitives and had little love lost on Ames or Butler. Cole sought them out, and plans for the robbery were laid.[39]

September 7, 1876, began as another quiet, routine day. Adelbert Ames penned a letter to Blanche, who had taken a trip to Lowell, Massachusetts: "Our miller has been away on a wedding tour. He has just returned, but has not as yet settled down to business. If I do half of what I have in mind, I will have to stay here until next spring. I may fail in every effort."[40]

But whatever Ames had in mind, it would have to wait. Shortly before 2:00 P.M., on that very day, September 7, 1876, the Ames men—Jesse, Adelbert, and John, who had later lost an arm in the belting of the mill—were all in town.[41] They had just left a board meeting in the First National Bank in the Scriver Building and were walking towards the west-side mill, accompanied by Fanny Ames, John's young daughter. As they approached the bridge over the Cannon River, they noticed four men attired in white linen dusters riding toward them.

Fanny later recalled: "One of them said in a low voice, "'There is Governor Ames himself.' My uncle [Adelbert] said to father [Jesse]: 'Those men are from the South and are here for no good purpose. No one here calls me Governor.'"[42] (Ames was actually in error, as most Northfield citizens did refer to him as "governor" because of his leadership in Mississippi.)

When the Ames men and little Fanny reached the Ames Mill a few minutes later, a man rushed in shouting, "They're robbing the bank!" The men then hurried back across the bridge in the direction of the First National Bank. Adelbert Ames described the situation in the street: "You can little appreciate the excitement in this town. Every old musket, shot gun, and pistol was drawn from its hiding place."[43]

Adelbert Ames dispatched a letter to Blanche the following day: "Yesterday this town was the scene of a very remarkable tragedy. Your letter of yesterday was written immediately after dinner, and I took it at once to the mill to be mailed. I had been at the mill but a few minutes when someone rushed in and reported that the bank was being robbed. This was about two o'clock. Going to the door, I heard rapid firing across the bridge. I walked over and made my way across the square to the corner of the stone building occupied by Mr. Scriver. As I went I saw quite a number of the citizens hiding behind houses and a few firing up the street towards or in the direction of our house. Going to the corner I found that it, the corner, was being raided . . . by someone and that those, as I went up, had run away excepting one man. I looked around the corner with that man who had a rifle, and as we were warned by those on the other side of the street, we both left."[44]

Ames also wrote: "The killing of Republicans by a set of Mississippi K.K.K. produces a similar state of sensation as the murdering of a number of men by Missouri cut-throats who are after plunder."[45]

Adelbert Ames considered himself the focus of the unsuccessful robbery attempt when he wrote, "Yesterday reminded me of an election in Mississippi. Is it not strange that Mississippi should come up here to visit me?"[46]

A southern Minnesota newspaper corroborated Ames's conclusion: "One reason for going there [Northfield] was the amount of money in the bank, and some of the boys had a grudge against the ex-governor of Mississippi, who was supposed to be interested in it."[47]

Adelbert Ames was frightened when he heard a report that the robbers had gone to the home of his brother. Undoubtedly, fear of retribution on the part of the gang for his "Southern carpetbagging," affected not only Adelbert but the entire Ames family as well.

"Soon word came that the robbers had gone to John Ames's house. This word was on the street for a few minutes when I met John in great trouble. He said they had gone to his house, and he must go up and look after his daughters. I told him they would not harm them at such a time and counseled calmness. No, he was going to look after his daughters. We were walking up the road to his house when someone coming back said they had gone and went as far as Dundas. John was put much at ease but still he was going on to attend to his girls and calm them with assurances of their safety. As the people were looking to him I made him turn back and went to his house myself. Arriving there I found they were not excited as they knew nothing of the facts."[48]

Ames wrote of the incident to his wife: "My criticism, quite uncalled for, to be sure, is that though seeming to be half frightened to death, she was really enjoying herself right royally." He also wrote about his father, Captain Ames, and brother John T., and how they had reacted through the whole of that terrible day: "John T. Ames was the ruling spirit in town—he and Father [Captain Ames]. The people did about as they said—especially Father; he is just the coolest man at such a scene of excitement I ever saw."[49]

But if the Ames family in Northfield was in fear of retribution from the robbers, it was not limited to that city only. Blanche Ames was visiting the family estate in Lowell, Massachusetts, at the time of the robbery, and, after receiving news of the tragedy in a letter from her husband, she wrote back immediately: "Father brought us word tonight of your trouble in Northfield with a band of roughs. You will begin to think that Mississippi manners have followed you North."[50]

Blanche elaborated upon her own fears, which she felt may have been connected to the robbery and the robbers' hatred of the Butler and Ames families: "It was raining this evening and very dark. I had been out through the billiard room, which was unlighted, and noticed through the open window in a passage that the light was streaming brightly through the parlor window onto the fern bed. With the thought in my mind that I would go down and turn off the gas as the rain would be likely to keep away all visitors, I put my head out of the window. There at the dining room door, looking through the slats at the girls clearing off the table and putting away the silver, was a man. He had an umbrella under his arm, a dark coat and light pants on. I thought at first it must be Father or Major, and yet why should they be looking through the slats in that manner. I called, 'Is that you, Father?' The man did not answer, but drew back behind the pillar. He could not see me owing to the intense darkness. His figure would have been invisible but for the light from the windows. He could only judge the direction of the voice. I called again, 'Can't you answer, what are you doing there, what do you want?' I was a little excited and spoke quick and sharp. While I was asking the questions, he had jumped from the piazza and disappeared. I went down to the library and asked Uncle Parker, who was there with Father, if he had brought anyone up with him. He said, 'No,' and started out to look for the man but returned after blowing his little whistle, saying that it was too dark to see anything. I then went into the kitchen and started up the three men, who were playing cards. They searched about but could find no one. The upshot was I concluded I should feel safer to have a loaded pistol ready for use."[51]

Ames joined his wife Blanche in New York City three years after the Northfield raid where he supervised the selling of flour from the Ames Mill. In 1879, thirty-five feet were added to the height of the Ames Mill, making it five stories high from the basement. Steam power via an Atlas Corliss Engine of 200 horse-power was added. A complete transformation of the grinding machinery was carried out, implementing ten double sets of Ellis' corrugated rolls, nine double sets of Smith's rolls, two single sets, one set of Stevens' scratch rolls, four centrifugal rolls, seventeen Smith's purifiers, twenty-five reels, three run of stones, with smutters, cockle machines, and other apparatus found in first class mills.[52]

The mill was soon manufacturing 400 barrels of quality flour in four hours. The water-power was provided from a head of nine feet on the Cannon River, and was transmitted by a pair of Victor turbine wheels, forty-eight inches in diameter. The mill was the first in the state to turn out the new process flour.

When the Spanish-American War erupted in 1898, Ames returned to the army as a brigadier general of Volunteers and served in the Santiago Campaign in Cuba. He was mustered out the following year.[53]

In 1917, he sold the Northfield mills to the L.H. Campbell Company, Malt-O-Meal, resold two years later to John C. Campbell.

The Ames' owned a beautiful mansion on "the Hill" in Tewksbury, Massachusetts, but Adelbert spent his winters in Ormond Beach, Florida, playing golf with his friend, John D. Rockefeller.

Adelbert and Blanche had six children, two sons and four daughters. Following Adelbert's death on April 13, 1933, two of the daughters—Jessie and Blanche—wrote biographies of Ames and the family: *Chronicles from the 19th Century and Adelbert Ames, Broken Oaths and Reconstruction of Mississippi, 1835-1933*.[54]

The ninety-seven-year-old Adelbert Ames was the last surviving full-rank general officer of the Civil War. Following his death, J.R. Lewis wrote a letter to the *New York Times*: "He was the last leaf on the tree, and he must have been the last prominent figure of one of the most stirring periods in our history. Possibly the rush of modern times makes the figures of a past age increasingly less concern to us."[55]

George Bradford

GEORGE BRADFORD WAS ONE OF THE CAPTORS of the Younger brothers. He was born near Patriot, Indiana, June 28, 1847, and arrived in Minnesota twenty years later. At the time of the Northfield bank robbery, he worked as a farmer, schoolteacher, and clerk of the courts in St. James. He was also a storeowner. When the fleeing Youngers reached Watonwan County, he was one of the first to respond to the call for men to serve on the posse.

George Bradford later recalled: "I had been sent out into the country the 21st day of September [1876] to take care of some business matters pertaining to the store and did not arrive back [at] the village until after the report was out that the robbers were in the vicinity. I at once saddled a horse and rode westward from the town and up the north side of the North Branch of the Watonwan River.

As I proceeded I met several men who informed me that the robbers had been driven to cover in the brush on the river. I passed on up to a point on the river opposite the home of one Andrew Anderson. Finding that the men were in the brush on the south side of the river, I crossed and gave my horse in care of a man and went forward to the edge of the bluff. Soon after, Captain W.W. Murphy and Benjamin Rice came to me and proposed that we get a squad of men and go down into the thicket and take the robbers out. I agreed to this, and we went down to a draw and on down into the river bottom where we stopped."[56]

Bradford also penned: "We were to march to the river, then wheel to the left and march slowly until we could see them. Soon after we started up the river, I became convinced that we were getting away from the river and leaned down to look under the brush and told Mr. Glispin that I thought he was getting away from the river—when something drew my attention to the front and, glancing that way, saw some of the men we were after, and just then one of them [Pitts] jumped up and fired.

"I had raised my gun to shoot, when a bullet struck, or rather grazed, my wrist and disturbed my aim, so it was a second or so before I fired," Bradford said. "Several shots were fired from both sides and a volley from across the river, from parties there. They could not see us from there but fired, the bullets cutting the twigs over our heads."[57]

George A. Bradford recalled Bob Younger walking slowly forward from the thicket holding high a white handkerchief in his left hand: "The ground along the river was quite undulating, and the robbers had been in a low settle. Bob came up onto the higher ground when told to come to us, and a man shot from across the river striking Bob under the arm, cutting the flesh. He stopped, and when told to come on, he said he had been shot from across the river. Murphy then called to them to cease firing as the men had surrendered. As Bob had said, the rest were all down, but Cole first got up, then Jim."

The robbers were taken to the second floor of Flanders House where Cole and Jim were given beds on the east end. Bob was put in a room on the west side. Parties of five and six men were permitted to enter the hall and gaze upon the wounded robbers. The visitors, however, could remain but a few minutes and were made to leave in order to make room for as many more.[58]

"I was placed with Bob and was with him all night," remembered George Bradford. "He was very careful what he said regarding their identity or of their movements. But I was told that Cole had told them who he and his brothers were, but would not tell the names of any of the men with them on the attack on Northfield, except (sic) Pitts, the dead man."[59]

Bradford married Flora Cheney of Madelia one year after the robbery. George Bradford died in Portland, Oregon, in 1935.[60]

John Bresett

IN 1851, SAINT PAUL WAS A SPRAWLING frontier community, the upper terminus of the Mississippi River boat trade, a town of tradesmen and merchants serving the nearby logging industry and the settlers attracted by the land boom developing to the West. It was a violent town with violent men—adventurers, entrepreneurs, trappers, gamblers—with the excitement, recklessness, and disorders inherent in the process of growing. Streams of men, along with their crimes and vices, were unloaded from the river packets in a continuing, troublesome procession.

This was the year and the environment in which Alexander Marshall was appointed to enforce the laws of the Territory. His was perhaps a hopeless task, working single-handedly against mobs of toughs attracted to the lawless freedom of the frontier. By 1854, Marshall had resigned, Saint Paul was incorporated as a city, and

William Miller was appointed chief of police of the new department. Miller, with four patrolmen, waged a courageous but ineffectual campaign against the general lawlessness and disorder of Saint Paul. Out of sheer necessity, a jail was built in 1857 at the cost of $6,500. This jail replaced a rough structure of logs and weatherboard.

The full effect of the land boom was felt in 1857. Murder, robbery, and assault were commonplace. Prostitution and gambling were flagrant. The strength of the police force had been increased to twelve men, assisted by a forty-man unpaid "Vigilance Committee." The officers, however, were assaulted, harassed and overpowered by the hordes of marauding roughnecks.

The onset of the Civil War brought dramatic changes to Saint Paul. War conditions resulted in the reduction of river traffic, and the shortage of saleable merchandise soon brought the business life of the city nearly to a standstill. The nation was in the midst of a severe economic depression, which further contributed to the troubles of the people. Three-quarters of the police enlisted in the army and no funds were available to pay the rest. It was, therefore, necessary to disband the night police. A force of two hundred volunteers was organized to take their places. They were divided into four companies, each responsible for order in one separate section of the city. The deeds of these men are today forgotten, but certainly their demonstrated courage and dedication enabled the city to survive.

After Appomattox, a period of relative prosperity prevailed. The long-suffering Vigilance Committee was replaced by Chief Michael Cummings and twelve patrolmen.

One of the early police detectives was John Bresett, who gained prestige with his quick response to the 1876 Northfield bank robbery. Bresett and his posse quickly took up the chase of the Northfield robbers. Hurrying to beat a Minneapolis posse led by Mike Hoy to the outlaws, Bresett lost little time in picking up their trail. A dispatch was relayed from Captain Rogers at 7:15: "Emery is just in from the German church on the Cleveland road through Elysian Township. He says the robbers have taken the road due west. St. Paul detective John Brissette [sic] and fifty men are in sight of and after them. Two are known to be wounded and another apparently wounded. George James shot at these men as they crossed the river at noon and thinks his man is wounded. Baxter and his crowd are with Brissette."[61]

Also with Bresett was Sheriff William H. Dill of Winona. With a force of 120 men, Dill had set up picket lines along the Winona & St. Peter Railroad tracks from Janesville to Meriden. The robbers, however, were not sighted. On September 11, a Dr. Cummings and a companion named Sackett discovered the robbers's trail near Long's Mills at German Lake. The trail paralleled an unused road leading southwest and revealed tracks of six or seven horses. In no place did the tracks approach the road to within five feet or less. The two men were certain the tracks corresponded to the description of those made by the robbers. Dill, joined by Bresett, followed the trail with some twenty men.[62]

That evening, the rainstorm grew worse with a wind coming in from the northeast. The rain did not let up through the night and the showers continued until midway through Monday. The rain helped the robbers's flight by obliterating their tracks, but it couldn't have been pleasant. Although 200 men surrounded the robbers, many of them were so disgusted with their own soaked condition, they abandoned their picket posts and left the roads and bridges unguarded. The party under the leadership of Bresett tracked the robbers to a point south of German Lake but then lost them.[63]

But special telegrams continued to be wired to the *St. Paul Dispatch*: "Brissette [sic] and Baxter with about fifty men have followed the robbers to Lake Elysian, where they have them corralled. It is thought here that every one of the gang will be shot or captured before night."[64] But the boys were not corralled, shot or captured—at least not this time.

When petty criminal—soon to be outlaw—George Sontag escaped from reform school on May 29, 1880, and went into hiding, word reached Bresett. Sontag later claimed he spent but four to six weeks in reform school before his escape, but his memory failed him or he deliberately lied, for he spent about five and a half months there.[65]

Authorities at the school made several attempts to return him to the school but failed to locate him. Sheriff John Bresett of St. Paul, who had gained fame as the "capital pet" for his steady pursuance of the Younger brothers following the Northfield Raid, was called upon to arrest George. The warrant was placed in the hands of Chief of Police Robinson, who made the arrest and turned the boy over to Bresett, who in turn, returned him to jail.[66]

Alonzo E. Bunker

ALONZO E. BUNKER WAS BORN IN LITTLETON, New Hampshire, on March 29, 1849, the second son of Enos A. and Martha M. Bunker. He was educated in Dodge County, Minnesota, and learned the printing business in Mantorville. Mr. Bunker served as a schoolteacher before attending the St. Paul Business College, from which he graduated in 1869. He commenced studies at Carleton College in 1871 and began working at the First National Bank of Northfield in 1873, where he remained for five years. In 1875, Alonzo Bunker married Nettie L. Smith of Red Wing.

On September 7, 1876, Mr. Bunker, upon hearing footsteps in the lobby, turned from his work to wait upon his customer. He found three men holding revolvers pointed at him and was ordered to throw up his hands. At first, Bunker thought some of his friends were playing a joke on him, but before he could comment, the three men jumped over the counter and covered the three employees with their weapons.

While Charlie Pitts and Frank James were intimidating Heywood, Bob Younger again turned his attention to the other two bankers. When Bunker had first thrown up his hands, he was still holding the pen he had been using when the robbers entered the bank. When he went to set it down, Bob Younger leaped at him and stuck his revolver into his face, telling him to keep his hands up or he'd kill him.

Younger then ordered the two bank employees to get on their knees behind the counter. Bob shifted his revolver from Bunker to Wilcox, then fumbled through papers on the counter top and in drawers. While on his knees, Bunker remembered the Smith & Wesson .32 caliber pistol on the shelf.

"I turned to see if I was near enough to reach the weapon, while Bob's back was turned to me, but Pitts happened to be looking my way at the time, and rushing across the intervening space, secured the revolver himself, and coolly stuffed it into his pocket," recalled Bunker.[67]

Bunker stumbled to his feet thinking he must try and make some kind of defensive action or at least break away, get outside and sound the alarm. Bob Younger turned to him again and barked, "Where's the money outside the safe? Where's the cashier's till?" Bunker pointed to a box with partitions in it sitting on top of the counter, which contained less than $100 in nickels, pennies, and a little silver. He replied, "There's the money outside."

Below the box, underneath the counter, was a drawer containing about $3,000 in currency. Bunker did not mention this money nor did Bob Younger find it. Again, the outlaw ordered Bunker to get back down on his knees and keep his hands up. Reaching into his linen duster, Bob pulled out a grain sack and began transferring the money from the cash box to the bag. After dropping in a couple of handfuls, it suddenly occurred to him, according to Bunker, that "the claim he was working, panned out but little."

Seeing Bunker still on his feet, Bob yelled, "There's more money than that out here. Where's that cashier's till? What in hell are you standing up for? I told you to keep down." He then grabbed hold of the banker and pushed him to the floor. Bunker did not resist. In doing so, Bob felt a large pocket book in Bunker's pocket. "What have you got here?" the outlaw shouted, digging it out. After looking it over, he placed it back in the pocket, pressed his revolver to Bunker's temple and pushed him to the floor, again bellowing, "Show me where that money is, you sonofabitch, or I'll kill you."

Bunker was sure his time had come. Thoughts of his wife, his mother, and God flashed through his head as Bob continued to grip his shoulder. Seeing that the banker was too frightened to answer, the outlaw released him and began another fruitless search for money outside the safe. Bunker stood up once more and noticed blood trickling down Heywood's face and neck from the wounds inflicted by Pitts. Since Heywood was prostrate, Bunker supposed the bullet had entered his head and killed him.

As Bob re-examined the contents of the drawer, Bunker started an escape move, despite the outlaw's gun pointed directly at him. The banker reasoned if he could get to Manning's hardware store, located west of the bank and across the alley, fronting Mill Square, the rear door of which was at right angles to the bank's rear door, he could sound the alarm. Of course, what was happening in the street might present another problem.

Wilcox was on his knees between Bunker and the door. Bunker motioned to him with his hand to move a little forward so he might be able to pass by. Suddenly Bunker dashed by him, and, as he approached the doorway, Pitts with a whoop fired at him from the side of the vault. The bullet whizzed past Bunker's ear and through the blinds on the door. Bunker dashed out the rear door through what he later called, "the best opening for a young man I have ever seen." The weight of his body sprang the blinds as he crashed against them. Turning to the left outside, he descended some steps to the alley. But Pitts was in hot pursuit. Bunker pivoted again at the bottom of the stairs when a second shot from Pitts ripped through his shoulder as he ran opposite the rear entrance of Manning's store.

The shot had been fired from twenty feet away. It hit the fleeing banker's shoulder, barely missing the joint. The bullet passed through the shoulder blade and exited just below the collarbone, within half an inch of the subclavian artery. Dazed, Bunker remained on his feet. Unsure as to his condition, Bunker did not jump into Manning's, but continued west instead through an open lot to Water Street and another block south to the home of a Dr. Coon.

Alonzo Bunker described an incident that occurred during his flight to freedom: "Mrs. John T. Ames was driving in her phaeton, and as she arrived on the corner of Water and Fifth Streets, near Dr. Coons, someone warned her of the danger, and she could hear the popping of revolvers. She alighted from her carriage, and as I passed her on my way from the bank to Dr. Coons, she was frantically running around her horse and phaeton, screaming lustily, "Oh, John! John! Where's John? Oh, I want John!"[68]

George Huntington later wrote of Bunker: "The part taken by Mr. Bunker in the encounter with the robbers in the bank . . . shows him to be a man of nerve, cool and self-collected in danger, and capable of bold action. Though not subjected to the brutal treatment inflicted upon Mr. Heywood, he was subjected to a similar temptation to secure his own safety by yielding to the demands of the robbers; and he kept such possession of his faculties; mental and physical, as to seize the first opportunity—an opportunity not afforded to Heywood—to break from his captors and escape under fire. The wound he received at that time was a dangerous one, and narrowly missed being fatal . . ."

In 1878, Mr. Bunker resigned his position at the First National and accepted a similar position in the Citizens Bank of Northfield. He served as a banker in Kansas City and St. Paul before moving to Helena, Montana, in 1882 where he organized the Second National Bank. In 1888, he returned to work for the Newspaper Union and moved to Chicago.[69] He died August 3, 1929, in Los Angeles.

Sherman E. Finch

WHEN THE FLEEING BANDITS WERE REPORTED to be in the area of Waterville and Elysian, Sheriff Sherman E. Finch of Mankato organized a party of eighteen to twenty good men and took to the woods. The roads were very poor, and because of the unending rain, they did not reach Janesville until morning.

Finch, Pope, E.F. Everitt, Captain Holmes, Andrew Anderson, Eric Olson, and three others—Robeson, McGraw, and Perry—reached Eagle Lake Station. The latest dispatches placed the robbers in the Janesville area, heading in their direction. The party started for Elysian, three of the men on horses on the north road of Madison Lake and six in carriages on the south fork.[70]

About seven o'clock that evening, a Mr. Warner, who lived two and a half miles north of Elysian, found the posse and related that the fleeing robbers were near his farm. The posse stationed guards at three different points to watch for the robbers in the pelting rain.

The following morning, Sheriff Finch and General Pope searched the Waterville-Cleveland Road but found no trace of the horses. They returned to Warner's farm. Eric Olson, accompanied by a Faribault man, investigated the Watonwan Road as far as Elysian. His companion had sighted the robbers one day earlier on this same road and pursued them until he lost the trail. Olson reported to Finch that all was quiet.

Several groups of men scoured the woods and discovered tracks in some areas but quickly lost them again. The men came to the conclusion that the robbers had passed that way before they had come on duty the night before. More tracks were found on the farm of a Mr. Ray, east of the lake, one mile northeast of Elysian. The posse followed the tracks due north towards the Marysburg Road, but in encountering some hunters, they retreated one mile northeast.

Towards evening, the party started back for Eagle Lake, searching several roads in small groups. When a large group of men arrived on the Winona & St. Peter Railroad, the picket line was expanded from the Wardlaw Ravine to the Waseca County line. Monday the whole force took the train back to Mankato.

That same afternoon, Finch, McGraw, Everitt, Holmes, Taylor, Olson, and a Northfield man departed Eagle Lake, all heavily armed. The group split up and followed two roads into Marysburg, where it was reported the robbers's camp had been discovered. In reaching the camp, the posse was unable to follow the tracks of the fleeing outlaws.

The robbers spent that night on an island in a marshy area. Under cover of darkness, they abandoned their horses and continued their flight on foot. At daylight, they reached the town of Marysburg and, in fear of being seen, made a circle around the town, walked another four miles south before they camped. Nine miles west of their camp, they walked up to a deserted farmhouse two or three miles from Mankato. The farmhouse, situated in a lonely forest, constituted a perfect hideout, and they remained two days and nights.[71]

Finch's party explored the island in the slough, and in locating the peculiar boot heel, the lawmen were certain the robbers were moving in a southwesterly direction. The posse returned to Mankato once again. The party was immediately informed that the robbers had been seen by A.L. Davis three miles south of town. The posse rode out to the LeSueur River Bridge, at Kerns, where a strong guard was placed. The main party proceeded along the Central railroad line in the Rapidan prairie. Sheriff Finch and five men guarded the wagon road leading to Red Jacket, and Major Rose, with four men, guarded the rail line all night in heavy rain. A force came over from Good Thunder to guard the area between the rail line and the Blue Earth River, but they were unable to stand the heavy rains and went home during the night.[72]

As the Finch party returned to the LeSueur Bridge, a courier brought news that the robbers had been seen at the farm of Henry Shabut, three miles north of town. The posse galloped through town, rode up through Thompson Ravine, left their horses at the farm of Peter Hoerr and proceeded on foot through the deep timber until dusk.[73]

On their way once more, the fugitives came to the county bridge over the Blue Earth River which they found well-guarded. About a quarter-mile beyond, however, they crossed the river on a railroad bridge and easily made their way in the darkness around the city of Mankato. But they had been seen crossing the river. The alarm was given and all available men in Mankato mustered. The pursuers, however, had to wait for daylight.[74]

Finch's party from Mankato rode through the night, determined to catch the outlaws. General Pope again joined the posse and had Eric Olson accompany Finch to Van Brunt's Slough as he expected the robbers to pass there. Some of Finch's guards had heard whistling emanating from the Pottery Ravine, and the lawmen believed the sounds might be signals of the outlaws. Mike Hoy and his party had already left for the ravine.[75]

Finch and Olson arrived at the bridge crossing the slough and were told by mounted guards that the outlaws had already passed through the slough. Finch ordered the guards to stay where they were as he was afraid that, should they pursue the bandits, they would wipe out their tracks.

Returning to Mankato, a small conclave was held between Finch, Olson, Davis, and Roberts at the foot of Liberty Street. General Pope sent the party back out to the slough where they picked up the outlaws's trail once more. Finch posted guards at the bridge, ordered them to not allow anyone to pass, and returned to Mankato to report to General Pope.

After Mike Hoy failed to capture the outlaws at Minneopa Falls and left to again attempt to pick up their trail, the Mankato party followed, and, near the Blue Earth River, Sheriffs Finch and Davis dismounted and took the trail on foot. The others led the horses along the wagon road. A courier met the party at South Bend and related that the robbers were surrounded. The group galloped quickly to Minneopa Falls but found no trace of the "surrounded" party, despite scouring the timber between the Blue Earth and Minnesota Rivers, as far west as Rush Lake.

Finch served as Blue Earth County Sheriff 1876-1877.

JOHN KOBLAS

Sheriff James Glispin

SHERIFF JAMES GLISPIN WAS SERVING HIS third term as sheriff of Watonwan County at the time of the Northfield bank robbery. He was a Civil War veteran with a reputation for settling trouble without violence. When reports circulated that the robbers were in the Janesville area, an army regiment divided into companies and joined the search as more reinforcements arrived. Meeting them at Janesville was a St. Peter contingent led by Mayor Strait and sixteen others, as well as another force commandeered by Sheriff James Glispin of Madelia.[76]

Sheriff Glispin's party rode toward the site given him by Sorbel, after leaving orders to his subordinates to form a large posse and follow him. Stores were boarded up, and most males rode out after him. A few miles from Madelia, Glispin met a rider who told him the robbers were to the southwest about four miles. Glispin and his men galloped in the direction of the bandits, and only one hour after getting the news from Sorbel, overtook the fugitives as they crossed a slough south of Lake Hanska.[77]

The Watonwan River, where the boys were holed up, was the principal stream in the area and ran from west to east. Several smaller streams served as tributaries, causing the topography of the area to be somewhat more broken that other parts of Watonwan County.[78]

Glispin's party, although cautious, moved toward the outlaws who were groping their way through the slough. Glispin ordered the robbers to halt, but his demand was ignored. The posse fired on them, but none of the shots hit any of the fleeing outlaws. Pursuing, Glispin and his small party sighted them again. Dr. Overholt fired at Cole Younger but missed, although he did hit his walking stick, breaking it in two. The robbers sighted some horses, but the Madelia posse positioned themselves between the fugitives and the mounts. The outlaws saw some men in buggies and briefly decided to steal their horses, but the men were armed with shotguns, and the boys changed their minds.[79]

The horsemen in both Glispin and Murphy's parties found the swollen slough impassable by horseback. After seeing the bandits run to the river and disappear, Glispin was joined by four well-armed farmers, and the tiny group divided itself and rode the perimeters of the slough. As Glispin's men found their way on horseback past the slough, the Youngers and Pitts ran two miles to the south, about three quarters of a mile from the river. When Glispin and his men were within a hundred yards of the robbers, one of the fugitives bellowed, "What do you want?"

Glispin answered, "Throw up your hands and surrender."[80]

As the robbers resumed their foot race, Glispin opened fire. The bandits fired back while in retreat, and their aim forced Glispin and his men to dismount and take cover in the underbrush. Just as the robbers disappeared into the brush, Cap Murphy's posse arrived from Madelia, and Glispin quickly had all the men dismount and form a skirmish line. Moving forward, the posse reached the river just as the robbers were scurrying up the bank on the opposite side.

Dropping to one knee, Glispin fired back, hitting Charlie Pitts. As the man fell, he was riddled by bullets from the men on the skirmish line.[81]

Glispin shouted out to the bandits to come out with their hands up and they would not be harmed. When Bob Younger emerged from the thicket with his one good arm held high, an overanxious posse member fired, hitting the outlaw under the arm.

Bob was shocked that someone had shot him while he was surrendering, especially since Glispin and the others had promised them protection. Glispin, also in shock over one of his men disobeying orders, then shouted he would shoot the first man who harmed any of the prisoners. Slowly advancing toward the wounded outlaws, the posse men helped Bob to his feet.

Bob agreed to reveal their true identities to Sheriff Glispin. When the lawman arrived at the Flanders House, Bob admitted that he had been one of the men in the bank at Northfield, but gave his name as George Huddleston, remarking that this was the name found on all the hotel registers.

Cole said he had planned on stealing some horses and wagons in their line of retreat, but Glispin, one step ahead of them, had them removed to a safe place.

Judson Jones of Madelia induced Glispin to close all the saloons in the city so the mob would not get drunk. Jones then went into the jail and informed the Youngers that everything was being done to protect them. Cole replied in a very dramatic voice, "Coming events sometimes cast their shadows before."[82]

Sheriff Glispin informed Cole that, "If they do come and I weaken, you can have your pistols."[83]

Glispin served a fourth term as sheriff following the Younger capture.

On Tuesday, April 10, 1880, the following article was published in the *Mankato Weekly Review*: "A man who gives his name as Edwards and his residence as the United States was convicted at St. James on Friday morning last, of an assault upon Sheriff Glispin, having struck him with a bottle, and was sentenced to twenty days confinement in the Mankato Jail. He was brought to this city by Friday afternoon's train by Deputy Sheriff Foot.

"Just as the train was entering the city, and when near the Van Brunt slough, Edwards made an excuse to go into the water closet. He stayed longer than the deputy thought necessary, and when he opened the door to look after the prisoner he found that he had crawled out the window and saw his straw hat just as he jumped from the train which was going at about twelve miles an hour. The deputy followed as quick as possible, but the prisoner had a good start and it was feared had made good his escape.

"Night watchman Young came to the sheriff's assistance, and, after following the trail, it was found that Edwards had crept into the tall grass in the slough where he was captured, nestling close to the ground. He was then safely lodged in the jail, to serve out his sentence."[84]

Glispin left Madelia in 1880 and moved to California where he became a mercantile businessman. He went to Spokane, Washington, in 1883, where his reputation as a fist fighter and "fitness for official life" put him in the public eye. He served two terms as sheriff before going into the real estate business. James Glispin, who went blind in his last few years, passed away in 1890, only fourteen years after the Northfield bank raid.

Joseph Lee Heywood

MR. HEYWOOD WAS BORN AT FITZWILLIAM, New Hampshire, August 12, 1837. At about the age of twenty, he left home and moved to Concord and Fitchburg, Massachusetts. In 1860, he moved on to New Baltimore, Michigan, where he worked for a year as a clerk and bookkeeper in a drugstore. Heywood moved to Moline, Illinois, the following year before enlisting in the 127th Regiment Illinois Infantry in Chicago. He saw action on the battlefield at Vicksburg and took part in the capture of Arkansas Post on January 11, 1863. He was hospitalized for over-exertion and exposure and nearly died before being sent back to Illinois. Here he served as a druggist in the dispensary at Nashville until his discharge in May 1865.

After serving as a druggist in Faribault and Minneapolis, Joseph Lee Heywood moved to Northfield in the fall of 1867 and became a bookkeeper in S.P. Stewart's Lumber Yard. In 1872, he accepted the position of bookkeeper in the First National Bank of Northfield. Mr. Heywood also held the positions of city treasurer and treasurer of Carleton College for two years. "And no man in Northfield was more highly thought of than he by all who knew him, for business accuracy and faithfulness, as well as for his many social and moral good traits." Heywood was twice married; first to Martha Buffum Heywood, who gave birth to a daughter, Lizzie May, on April 25, 1871. After the death of Martha, shortly after Lizzie's birth, Heywood married a second time. Lizzie Adams married Heywood in 1874 and became Lizzie May's stepmother.[85]

Heywood was formerly of Minneapolis where he was in the employ of Captain John Martin. When the bank in Northfield had opened four years earlier, he accepted a position there, serving also as city-treasurer of Northfield and volunteer treasurer of Carleton College, a position for which he was not paid. Heywood had accomplished these positions regardless of being diagnosed as a hopeless consumptive ten years earlier.[86]

Inside the bank on that fateful day in 1876, the first three robbers startled the three bank employees: Alonzo E. Bunker, teller; Joseph Lee Heywood, bookkeeper; and Frank J. Wilcox, assistant bookkeeper. Since the cashier, George M. Phillips, was out of state, Heywood was serving as acting cashier. At the time, the bank was located in temporary quarters. A "store-type" counter stretched across two sides of the interior between the lobby and the room's interior. A tall railing with glass panels ran the entire counter length, but there was an open space, totally unprotected, where a man had ample room to pass through.[87]

Pointing a revolver at Heywood, one of the outlaws snapped, "Are you the cashier?"

Heywood claimed he was not.

The same question was put to Bunker and Wilcox, both of whom insisted they were not the cashier.

While demanding the opening of the safe, the robbers went through the pockets of the bank employees and looked for weapons. When Bob Younger's hand struck a large jack knife in Wilcox's hip pocket, he remarked, "What's that?" Assured it was only a jack knife, Bob left him alone. The outlaws searched the office for a cash drawer but found only an open till on the counter, from which they appropriated a handful of small currency. The money was put in a grain sack, which was left on the floor.

"You are the cashier," bellowed one of the robbers, focusing his attention upon Heywood, who was sitting at the cashier's desk and appeared to be the oldest. "Open that safe—quick, or I'll blow your head off."[88]

Charlie Pitts stepped into the open vault, when Heywood, getting up from the floor and protective of the contents, jumped to the vault door and attempted to close it upon him. He was quickly seized and dragged away from the door. Bob Younger noticed that Bunker had edged to the counter, and the outlaw jumped in front of him after noticing a small revolver on the shelf. He commanded Bunker to keep silent, and placed the revolver in his own pocket. Bob bellowed, "You couldn't do anything with that little derringer anyway."

Grabbing Heywood, the outlaws insisted he was the cashier. Said Wilcox: "As they stood over him, one pulled out a knife, drew Heywood's head back, and said, 'Let's cut his throat.' I think the knife was drawn across his throat leaving a slight scratch. Then to further intimidate him, a shot was fired over his head. About this time the leader ordered one of the others to go into the vault and try the safe. I believe it was Pitts who replied, 'All right, but don't let him [Heywood] lock me in there.'"[89]

The recollections of A.E. Bunker differ slightly from those of Wilcox. According to Bunker, Frank James and Charlie Pitts both grabbed Heywood when he attempted to close the door of the vault and pointed their revolvers in his face. He was told to "open that safe, now, or you haven't a minute to live."[90]

Recalled Bunker: "Heywood replied, 'There is a time lock on, and the safe can't be opened now.' 'That's a lie,' retorted James and Pitts, and repeatedly demanded that he open the safe, coupling each demand with a threat, and commenced hustling Heywood about the room. Seeming to realize they were desperate men, Heywood called 'Murder! Murder! Murder!' whereupon James struck him a terrible blow on the head with his revolver, felling him to the floor. Some think this would have killed Heywood had no other injury been inflicted. He fell perfectly limp, and could not have been fully conscious after receiving the shock, as no word escaped his lips. Pitts then drew a knife from his pocket, and, opening it, said: 'Let's cut his damned throat,' and drew the edge of the knife across poor Heywood's neck, inflicting a slight wound while he was lying helpless on the floor."[91]

The outlaw pair then dragged Heywood inside the vault and again ordered him to open it. At the same time, revolvers were leveled at Wilcox and Bunker, and they too were ordered to unlock the safe. The robbers did not know that the safe was not locked at the time. With the door closed, the bolts thrown in place, the outlaws could not tell that the dial was still tuned to the correct combination.

Growing angry, Pitts placed his revolver to Heywood's head and fired. The bullet struck a tin box of jewelry and valuable papers in the vault.

The last robber, presumably Frank James, began his move towards the door. Turning to go, he took a final glance at Heywood. After the robber leaped over the railing, he turned, aimed his revolver at Heywood's head and fired. Heywood staggered forward, the bullet lodged in his head, and fell behind the counter leaving a pool of blood on the matting.[92]

The blotter on Heywood's desk was smeared with blood and particles of brain, as was his desk. When the town's citizens entered the bank, they found the murdered man prone upon his face, blood and brains oozing from a hole in his right temple.

Among the first citizens to reach the bank was Myron W. Skinner, one of the town's leading merchants. Skinner later recalled: "Looking over the counter, I saw Mr. Heywood lying there dead, his head resting about where the paying teller usually stood. I helped carry him home to his wife. I then went to the telegraph office to telegraph to Dundas, in which direction the robbers had gone, what had been done here and ask them to intercept them, but the operator at Dundas [Homer Roberts] was not in, and the message could not then be sent. When I went home at night, my wife said to me that before she knew what to make of the noise, it sounded more like the popping of corn than anything else."[93]

Another account states that Heywood breathed for about twenty minutes but did not sleep before death took him.[94]

The scene inside the bank was no better with the bloodied body of Heywood on the floor. Since the Heywoods lived quite a distance from the center of town, his wife learned of the death by accident. Carleton College President James W. Strong was on his way to inform her of her husband's murder, but she had overheard a neighbor shout the news to another across the street. Although pained, the courageous lady, in hearing the grisly details of his death, said, "I would not have had him do otherwise." President Strong, meanwhile, did not complete his mission, turning back instead to accompany Heywood's body to their home.[95]

A friend referred to Heywood as a shy, well-liked young man and was deeply moved by his passing. She later recalled: "I don't think there was such a thing as an ambulance in town at that time, so they came for Mr. Heywood's body with a regular buggy. It was drawn up at the rear entrance of the bank. I saw the men carry out the body of poor Mr. Heywood and lay it in the buggy. Then they covered it over with a sheet."[96]

Reverend Leonard's funeral discourse included this tribute: "Mr. Heywood was beyond most men modest and timid. He shrunk from the public gaze, and, considering high gifts, and standing in the business community, was retiring almost to a fault. And yet he was never absent from the post of duty. He set a low estimate upon himself. He would not own to himself, did not even seem to know that he was lovable and well beloved, and was held in high esteem by all. He courted no praise and sought no reward. Honors must come to him unsought if they came. He would be easily content to toil on, out of sight and with services unrecognized, but with every transaction he must be conscientious through and through, and do each hour to the full the duties of the hour. . . . When so many are corrupt and venal, are base and criminal, in the discharge of public duties, the spectacle of such a life as we have looked upon is worth far more to society than we can well reckon up. And if, as a result of last Thursday's events, those just entering life, and we all, shall be warned of the evil and curse of transgression, and be reminded of the surpassing beauty of honor and faithfulness, and in addition shall catch an enthusiasm of integrity, it will go no way to compensate for the terrible shock that came to this city, and for the agony that has fallen upon so many hearts. We know today that public and private worth are still extant, and that the old cardinal virtues are still held in honor. We need no lantern to find a man."[97]

Joseph Lee Heywood left a wife and child to mourn his loss. At the time of Heywood's untimely death, Lizzie May was only five years of age. Lizzie Adams, second wife of Joseph Lee Heywood, and her stepdaughter, Lizzie May, left Northfield five months after the slaying in the bank and moved to Indianapolis, Indiana. Heywood's daughter, Lizzie May, did not lose touch with the bank as the institution's president, John C. Nutting, became her legal guardian and executor of a fund for Lizzie in memory of her father.⁹⁸

Lizzie May left Indianapolis in 1881 and moved in with her maternal grandparents in Worcester, Massachusetts, where she attended school. Three years later, Margaret Evans, the first dean of women at Carleton College, brought the thirteen-year-old Lizzie back to Northfield and assisted her in enrolling at the Carleton Academy, a college preparatory school. In 1889, upon completing above-average academic accomplishments, she entered Carleton College and continued to excel. An accomplished pianist, she graduated from Carleton with a B.A. in music and continued her studies at the Conservatory of Music in Indianapolis.

She returned to Northfield in 1897 to marry Edwin Carleton Dean in the home of her guardian, John C. Nutting. Settling in Scranton, Pennsylvania, she taught piano, served as secretary of the Scranton Daughters of the American Revolution and was a member of the Colonial Dames of America and the Daughters of the Founders and Patriots of America.

May's father was always in her heart. In 1923, she wrote an article for the *Carleton Daily News Bulletin* entitled "A Day with a College Treasurer." "And the baby—she had cried all day," wrote May. "She had wanted her father. Perhaps she had already sensed that very soon she would want her mother and then her father, oh very badly! Her father takes her and walks. All day he stood but now he walks! Of course the baby never stopped crying . . ."⁹⁹

Lizzie May passed away in 1947. A friend related, "Deep loyalty to Carleton was one of Mary Dean's chief characteristics. During the last fifteen or even twenty years of her life, she suffered from recurring illness and physical weakness. She leaves us a lesson of great bravery in the way she bore these burdens. Her endurance and courage and her loyalty to her college and to her friends were outstanding."¹⁰⁰

JOHN KOBLAS

Reverend Francis Howard

BORN IN VERMONT ON AUGUST 6, 1827, Francis Howard went on to serve as a corporal in Company H, First Regiment, Vermont Cavalry. Upon moving to Minnesota, he became pastor of the Baptist church in Union Lake where he remained for several years. After settling in Northfield, he served on the Board of Education for many years, maintaining a special interest in its affairs.[101]

About two o'clock on the afternoon of September 7, 1876, Francis Howard was standing at the west end of the bridge in Northfield when he noticed horsemen riding three abreast crossing the Cannon River Bridge.

"They attracted my attention by their dress and general appearance, and I turned and followed them across the bridge, probably a rod or a rod and a half behind," remembered Howard. "I followed them until about forty feet to the east of the bridge, where I met Elias Stacy, who stood on the sidewalk, looking at them. I was so near to them that when I spoke I had to speak very low so that they would not hear me. I said, 'Stacy, those gentlemen will bear watching,' and he replied that he thought so too."[102]

Howard and Stacy followed the riders up the street, but remained on the sidewalk. The riders proceeded to the corner where the bank was and tied their horses. The Northfield pair watched their movements from the opposite corner. The robbers then walked around to a store at the north side of the bank and sat down on a dry goods box. Two more riders soon rode up in front of the bank followed by three others who stopped in the center of the square on the north side. As soon as the trio stopped, the first three men got up from the dry goods box and entered the bank.

Howard quickly approached Allen and his companions and said, "There is a St. Alban's raid." The frightened Howard was referring to an 1864 Confederate raid led by Bennett Young on the town of St. Albans, Vermont. The gray-clad invaders had charged into town from Canada and planted the Confederate flag in the town square before being chased out by irate farmers.

"Mr. Allen, as soon as I made this remark, left us at once and went to the bank door and attempted to look in," recalled Howard twenty-one years later. "Immediately, a man stepped out from the doorway and caught Mr. Allen as I thought by the lapel of his coat, and drew his revolver and swung it over his head, began shooting in the air and shouting, 'Get out of there, you sons of bitches.' Mr. Allen broke away and ran rapidly towards where we were. As soon as the shooting commenced, the men on Mill Square also began shooting, and we got under cover as quick as we could. I went into the store on the corner and from there to the roof, and from my position there looked down on the street. When I looked, one of the robbers was lying dead in the street. Two of them were further south, reloading their revolvers, and when they got their weapons loaded, they came down the street on the run, shooting left and right without taking aim. That continued until the men came out of the bank and left town. They evidently were keeping the people back until they could get their men out of the bank and get away."[103]

Following the raid, Francis Howard became involved in local politics. In March of 1896, he penned a lengthy letter to the *Northfield News* concerning Primary Law. Objecting strongly to the rule restricting votes in the primary election of only one political party, Howard concluded: "Living, as I do, in the Third Ward of this city, and being one of the Republican committee of the ward, it is giving me a good deal of concern whether there will be enough Republicans left in the ward who did not vote at the late irregular caucus in this ward, so we can fill the offices even at a primary already called for on the 17th of this month."[104]

Reverend Howard, "held in high esteem and respect by everyone who knew him," passed away on June 12, 1901. He had been a member of Heywood Post, Grand Army of the Republic, whose members served as his pallbearers.[105] Services were at his residence.[106]

JOHN KOBLAS

Michael Hoy

MICHAEL HOY WAS BORN IN 1837. He married Catherine Quealy (1839 to 1926) in Hennepin County in 1860 and settled at 703 Main Street Northeast in St. Anthony (now Minneapolis). Catherine and her sister Honorah Quealy were living on the Eagan farm with Patrick Quealy and Margaret Gorman before their weddings. The Quealy family emigrated from County Clare—from the area of Haugh's Cross in Lisheencrony about five miles by road from Kilkee.

During the Civil War, Mike Hoy fought for the Union Army, and during the Battle of Nashville, he received a bullet wound above the wrist, which nearly entirely disabled his entire arm. Hoy was promoted from first lieutenant to captain on the field for gallantry in action. He joined Company K., Tenth Minnesota, Captain J.H. Baker commanding, on the 22nd day of August 1862 and served until the 16th day of December 1864.[107]

Captain Hoy belonged to the St. Anthony volunteer fire service for seventeen years, and was foreman of the Minnesota Engine Company for four years. He was elected city marshal (east division) in the summer of 1867 and filled that position for seven years, until St. Anthony became consolidated with Minneapolis. In him, during this period, was centered the entire criminal and police system. He was also a deputy sheriff. For over two years, he conducted all the criminal business of Hennepin County and a great portion of it for many years after. After the consolidation, he was appointed chief of police, under Mayor George Brackett. [Brackett later went to the Yukon Territory and gained fame as a stampeder. In 1897, he witnessed the carnage and horror of the White Pass Trail. Scarcely a single horse survived of the three thousand that were used on the trail. Finally, it was closed to all, and Brackett began to construct a wagon road along the mountainsides. When it was completed, the stampeders who followed in the winter were glad to pay a toll to use it, but each one who passed that way was haunted in some fashion by the ghosts of the pack animals that had died that fall.][108]

After the chief of police appointment, he held the position of chief of detectives under Mayor Eugene McLanahan Wilson, who was elected mayor of Minneapolis in 1872 and 1874. Later Hoy was appointed a police commissioner by the council and served for two years as vice-president of that body. Captain Hoy was also appointed deputy U.S. marshal by President Grover Cleveland, which position he held until October 1890.[109]

While Captain Hoy served as marshal, there in the county but one small structure used as a jail, located near Central Avenue between Fifth and Sixth streets. Commonly referred to as "Hoy's little stone jug," it was the only lockup west of St. Paul. When prisoners were committed for any prolonged period, they were taken to St. Paul, the county paying for their maintenance, as there was no place to keep them elsewhere. Sometimes "Hoy's little stone jug" would be filled to overcrowding, and if there were any females among the unfortunates, they were placed apart from the male prisoners in one of the two rooms that served for the lock-up. The duties of the jailor (Marshal Hoy) were simple enough. He merely turned the key on them and went about his business. Sometimes in the morning on his return he would find his little stone jug empty, the inmates having escaped. After a time, a high fence was built around the jail and the escapes were less numerous in consequence. Later a new lock-up was located under the court house (west side) at Eighth Avenue South and Fourth Street.

Hoy's law enforcement career may be best known for his failed attempt to arrest the fake Lord Gordon Gordon in Winnipeg, Manitoba, in 1873. The bogus lord had swindled financier Jay Gould and others out of some capital and succeeded in getting across the border to take refuge in Winnipeg, although his whereabouts were unknown for nearly a year. A.F. Roberts, one of Gordon's victims, learned that the swindler was in hiding at Fort Garry. Gould's lawyers prevailed upon Minneapolis Mayor George A. Brackett to dispatch an officer to Canada to retrieve Gordon. Bracket chose Hoy for the job. "Physically he was big and strong, and mentally he was alert, resolute and courageous." Hoy was permitted to choose an assistant, and he quickly selected Owen Keegan, a friend who had formerly served on the Minneapolis police force.[110]

Hoy was given $200 in cash, a letter of credit for a thousand dollars, and a document labeled "Instructions." Loren Fletcher, a member and later speaker of the Minnesota House of Representatives, happened to be in Winnipeg on business. Hoy's instructions were to present all letters to Fletcher and not to wait for baggage should they encounter Lord Gordon.

With characteristic determination to get his man, Captain Hoy, with Keegan, proceeded to Winnipeg on June 26th and arrived on the stage from Breckenridge on July 2nd. Hoy also carried a letter addressed to L.R. Bentley, a Winnipeg merchant, who had pledged to help capture "one of the most outrageous scoundrels on the continent."[111] Fletcher and Bentley arranged with liveryman John R. Benson for a team and double-seated wagon which Bentley would drive.

Bentley and party rode out five miles to the residence of James McKay, just west of the fort. Leaving Hoy on the road, Bentley drove on to the McKay house and went in, pretending to be making a social call. Bently returned and took Fletcher in his wagon while Benson took Hoy and Keegan along a prairie road in back of the McKay house. Seeing Gordon seated on a veranda, Hoy and Keegan leaped from the wagon and physically dragged their prisoner to the main road while Benson reappeared with the wagon. The two police officers pulled Gordon into the wagon and seated him between them.[112]

Fletcher reappeared and jumped into the wagon. Because Hoy had lost his handcuffs in the scuffle, he pinioned Gordon's arms and legs with halter straps. As they neared the fort, Gordon demanded to see his counsel but was denied, as the wagon crossed the toll bridge over the Assiniboine River without paying the toll. After a bottle of whiskey was passed around, Bentley drove Fletcher back to town while Benson drove his three passengers toward the international border.

On July 3rd, when the expedition was but a few hundred yards from the international border, it was stopped by a British customs officer and his assistant, who was armed with a rifle. Only fifteen minutes earlier, the officer had received a telegram reading, "Five Americans kidnapped Gordon, commonly called Lord Gordon, and are running him out, it is supposed by your way. Arrest all parties if they can be found. Get all assistance necessary."[113]

Canadian authorities disputed this irregular practice of extradition, and Hoy plus his associate, Owen Keegan, were arrested and questioned over their requisition papers. Gordon was released and given Hoy's pistol to protect himself on his journey home, while Hoy and Keegan were sent to Winnipeg on a steamboat under guard.[114]

The following morning, Loren Fletcher and Minneapolis businessman, George N. Merriam, were traveling by private conveyance when they encountered the attorney-general of Manitoba, J.H. Clarke, on his way to Fort Garry accompanied by Gordon. Clarke informed Fletcher that he would be required to testify in the case of Hoy and Keegan. The next night, they were arrested and incarcerated at Fort Garry with Hoy and Keegan. The four prisoners were considered desperate criminals, allowed no physical exercise, and watched continually by guards. After receiving an urgent telegram from Fletcher, Minneapolis Mayor George Brackett hurried to Fort Garry.[115]

The preliminary examination commenced on July 8th before Judge Betourney of the Court of Queen's Bench. On the fifth day, the attorney general verbally attacked the American counsel, who had published an apologetic letter attempting to explain the arrest of Gordon in what was believed to have been strictly lawful. The letter was considered an outrage upon the citizens of Manitoba and a contempt of court.

After forty nights awaiting trial for "conspiracy to abduct a British subject from British soil," the four prisoners aroused excitement and sympathy at home. During that time public opinion in Minnesota soared, relations with Canada grew strained, and at last there was a movement to send a regiment of soldiers to secure their release. Political pressure brought about a plea bargain, and Hoy and Keegan were released.

On September 16th, Minnesota Governor Horace Austin telegraphed: "We leave for home tomorrow evening per steamer *Dakota* and take all the boys with us." A crowd of two thousand plus two marching bands and the Irish Rifles were present to welcome home the detainees on the morning of September 22nd. That evening, a dinner party was held in Brackett's Hall followed by a dance which lasted well into morning.[116]

In July 1874, Attorney General Clarke had occasion to pass through the state of Minnesota. Hoy, who hated the "brutal blackguard" for the ill treatment bestowed upon him, learned that his adversary was to be in St. Paul on July 20th. Hoy showed up there, too, and administered a severe physical beating to Clarke. Hoy was charged with "assault with intent to murder," waived examination and was released on $1,500 bail. No further proceedings were ever recorded. The following day, Lord Gordon, placed a pistol to his head and killed himself.

Following the Northfield bank robbery, Hoy and his posse pursued the James-Younger Gang and skirmished with them near Morristown. One newspaper reported that Hoy had been wounded in the exchange of gunfire, but it was later learned this report was incorrect.[117]

"One of the unfortunate features of the search is the rivalry be [sic] the police parties of St. Paul and Minneapolis," wrote Dr. McIntosh. "The rivalry between Hoy and Brissette [sic] is bitter, and they persistently refuse to cooperate. The defeat of the object sought to be obtained is the inevitable result."[18]

Minneapolis Detective Hoy and St. Paul's Bresett were competing to become the captor of the notorious outlaw band. While Bresett was tolerated, "the broth of a boy" Hoy was not popular with most Minnesotans.

Mike Hoy, however, was determined to keep up the chase. He and his men rode to the Conway house hoping to find the leader of the horse-thief gang at home. Conway was not at home, but a boy named Dolan, who had recently served a term in state prison for burglary, was forced to go along with the lawmen. Hoy placed a rope around the boy's neck, but the young man refused to talk. According to the *Minneapolis Tribune*, Conway was suspected of being the eighth man in the James-Younger Gang.

When the fleeing robbers were seen crossing the Blue Earth River near Mankato in 1876, posses in the area were alerted. The first party to take after the gang was led by Mayor Ames of Northfield, Detective Mike Hoy, and two other Minneapolis policemen. Hoy was at the Mankato House. He had gone no further than the bridge over Van Brunt's Slough and did not know the robbers had passed there. When he learned that the posse had picked up the robbers' trail at that location, he immediately wanted to be taken there, as he was not familiar with the country. Hoy, however, decided to go to the bridge with his own men.

It did not take Hoy and the others long to locate the robbers, when at about 6:00 A.M., they smelled smoke emanating from a dense wood near Minneopa Falls. Investigating immediately, Hoy and company climbed down from their mounts. As they pushed through the heavy underbrush, they heard the robbers scurrying up the opposite side of a ravine, although they could not see them through the bushes.

Meanwhile, a party of fourteen or fifteen men from Lake Crystal had come down on the early morning train and jumped off a mile or so west of Minneopa and had trudged through the thicket toward the falls, just as the Ames/Hoy party was on its way from Mankato. John Riley, one of the Lake Crystal party, later recalled: "The robbers were alarmed as they were getting their breakfast and left in their camp, part of a roast chicken, some green corn, a hat, and a rubber overcoat."[119]

Hoy's failure to capture the outlaws at Minneopa Falls was blamed upon his undisciplined posse members who rushed through the underbrush shouting. This action gave the outlaws a chance to escape across the Lake Crystal Road and lose themselves in the underbush. But some posse members, such as Eric Olson, blamed Hoy for the fiasco: "He was in such a hurry to get off that he did not have time to hear," recounted Eric Olson. "I told him to take it cool and lay his plans well before he started, but he rushed off with his men, and instead of following the trail, like on a deer hunt, carefully, and surround the fugitives, he let his men run a foot race past the robbers' camp, making a great noise, and then he discovered the camp the robbers had left. It is safe to say that Mr. Hoy's running so as to be the first to get the glory and reward was the cause of the robbers' escape there."[120]

Bob Younger later told a reporter during an interview that this statement was true. He once asked a reporter to point out Mike Hoy as he was curious to see what the man looked like. Hoy, however, was not present.[121]

Cole Younger also considered Hoy inept. On September 22nd, the day after his capture, he sent the following telegram to the *St. Paul Dispatch*: "We have surrendered. Mike Hoy can now come on with safety."[122]

Hoy was also condemned for striking fellow posse member Judson Jones for his negative comments on the actions employed by the posse at Minneopa Falls. Because Jones was in ill-health, Hoy was denounced in a local newspaper: "He can kick, beat and otherwise maltreat unarmed, defenseless men of weak physical condition, but he dare not follow the robbers in the brush. Bah! Brave little man that Hoy."[123]

Hoy came under criticism again from a Mankato newspaper: "If Hoy is bound to whip everyone who criticizes adversely his conduct in the pursuit of the robbers, he's got an all-winter's job before him. He can commence at Mendota, follow the Minnesota to South Bend, the railroad to Lake Crystal, and another railroad to Janesville, and the wagon road to Northfield, by the time he gets there he'll wish his fist was the jaw-bone of an ass, rather than the fist of one man. He'll do well enough to go with Fletcher on a kidnapping expedition to Manitoba, but as a robber hunter he's a failure."[124]

A Minneapolis newspaper stated, "Sheriffs Davis, Dill, etc., deserve fully as much if not more credit than the detectives who have endeavored to monopolize the glory."[125]

Two disgruntled posse members who had been involved in the siege at Minneopa complained of poor management of the hunt. The two men, named Rigby and Rehausen, charged, "All leaders, no followers."[126] Unmoved by the comments of so many, Hoy continued his pursuit of the robbers.

While most of the posses followed the trail of the two escaping James boys toward the South Dakota border, Hoy and his party continued searching along the tracks of the Sioux City Railroad near Linden. About daylight, they saw a light blue smoke rising out of the brush about ten rods from the tracks. Rather than encircle the robbers and send a man for additional help, Hoy's men dashed blindly into the woods, driving the fleeing bandits up a bluff known as Pigeon Hill.[127]

When Hoy's men attempted a pursuit, they found the outlaws had escaped once again through the dense underbrush. Returning to the outlaw camp, Hoy found some green corn and some nicely prepared chickens, which had been stolen nearby. In addition to the robbers' uneaten breakfast, the posse found two bridles, a linen duster, a handkerchief covered with bloodstains, and parts of a bloody shirt. The men knew at once that at least one of the robbers was wounded. Lost and turning in circles, the fleeing bandits pushed on through the thick swampland seven miles north of Madelia. That was the closest Hoy got.

The Hoys had nine children. Mike Hoy passed away in 1895. He and his wife, Catherine Quealy Hoy, are buried at St. Anthony Cemetery in northeast Minneapolis, Minnesota. Mike Hoy was immortalized in the popular poem, "The Robber Hunt," published originally in the *Winona Republican*, September 1876:

> "This is Mike Hoy, the broth of a boy,
> Who shouldered his little Winchester toy,
> To beat Brissette, the capital pet,
> Who swore, you bet, he'd have 'em yet,
> Then joined the men, that mounted then,
> To chase the six, who got in a fix,
> That's left of eight, who smelled the bait,
> That is, the malt, that lay in the vault,
> That was in the bank at Northfield."
>
> (excerpt)

Anselm R. Manning

ANSELM R. MANNING, NAMED FOR A second century Archbishop of Canterbury, was born near Montreal, Canada, and moved to Northfield in 1856. When the railroad was to pass through Northfield, he served as one of the surveyors. With business booming in Northfield, he started a stove and hardware store on Mill (Bridge) Square and prospered. He later became the proprietor of an ice-cutting and distributing business, as well. He served as assistant chief of the volunteer fire department, and was a member of the Episcopal Church and Masonic Lodge.[128]

Manning married May LaLanne on September 3, 1874, in Chicago.

In Northfield, during the 1876 robbery attempt, J.S. Allen, had run to A.R. Manning at the hardware store and told him of the robbery in progress. Manning quickly grabbed a rifle and some cartridges.

Manning, who was forty-two years old at the time of the raid, later recalled: "When I first heard the shooting, I thought these men had gotten permission from the  mayor to ride through the streets shooting blanks to call attention to a Wild West show (scheduled for later in the day). Then I heard someone shout, 'Robbing the bank.' I had been practicing with my rifle (a single-shot, breech-loading Winchester) the spring before and knew exactly what it would do, so I ran back and got it, stuffed a handful of cartridges in my pocket and ran back to the corner, loading on the way."[129]

"Very soon A.R. Manning came around the corner," recalled H.B. Gress. "Others were with him, but he seemed the leader and displayed more real nerve than all the robbers put together. He stood on the corner after the citizens had driven them south on Division Street and faced them all, not knowing but they might attack him from the rear. The robbers at that time were hollering to each other, 'Kill the white-livered son of a bitch on the corner,' referring to Manning."[130]

The *Martin County Sentinel* reported: "Manning next came out with a Remington repeating rifle, fired, Bates called, 'Jump back now, or they'll get you." J.B. Hide came and discharged both barrels of his shotgun. Rev[erend] Phillips 'took a turn at the scoundrels.' L. Stacey delivered a cool deliberate aim."[131]

Manning later recalled: "As I turned the corner going to the bank, I saw two men on the opposite side of their horse which was tied to a post. "I knew they were robbers the minute my eyes struck them. I drew my gun on them, and as I did so they doubled right down behind the horse. Without taking my gun from my face I lowered the muzzle and shot the horse."[132]

Manning added: "You may wonder why I did this, but I supposed they had come to sack the town . . . and were making breastworks of their horses."[133]

W.H. Riddell, who later co-founded the Northfield Furnace Company, observed the shooting of the horse: "Two of the robbers laid down behind the dead horse and commenced shooting north down the street while one of them was under the bank stairs," recollected Riddell. "One of those behind the dead horse jumped up and ran to the bank door and shouted, 'For God's sake, boys, hurry up: It is getting too hot for us."[134]

Manning quickly jumped around the corner to reload. In doing so, he found he could not pull the shell from his gun, but he ran swiftly back to his store and chucked a ramrod through the rifle releasing the shell. R.C. Phillips, another local citizen, had an explanation for the shell problem: "On the day of the Northfield raid I was in the shop working for A.R. Manning. My shop opened directly on an eight-foot alley from the back door of the bank. The first thing I heard was some loud talking in the bank, and then I heard a shot. When I heard the shot I started for the front of the store where Manning was working on his books. I asked Manning what that shot was, and he said, 'I think it's that show that's going to be here tonight.' I started to go up around the corner where the steps were, when I met John Tosney and John Archer who shouted, 'They're robbing the bank.' At that time five men whom I saw on the bridge started to drive rapidly across the square, firing right and left and shouting, 'Get in, you sons of bitches.' I ran back into the store, took the guns and revolvers we had and threw them out on the showcase, handing at the same time a single shot Winchester to Manning. In doing so, however, I made a mistake and gave him the wrong size shells, so that after he went out and attempted to load his rifle he found he had to come back to get new shells."[135]

But Manning returned to his position at the corner, again reloading as he ran. Seeing two or three robbers in front of the bank facing him, he fired a shot. The bullet hit a post, which supported some stairs, but in passing through the post, the bullet hit Cole Younger in the hip. [A few weeks later, a Faribault doctor extracted it and gave it to Manning, who carried it as a good luck charm].[136]

Manning was far from finished. Peeking around the corner, he found Bill Chadwell perched on his horse doing sentry duty some seventy to eighty feet up the street. The horseman had adapted the Indian tactics of hiding behind his horse's neck "and firing running fire."[137] More cautious now, Manning jumped back, reloaded and peeked around the corner. Taking deliberate aim, Manning fired. The bullet ripped through Chadwell's heart. The outlaw fell dead from his saddle, and the horse ran around the corner to a nearby livery stable.[138]

Manning recalled: "When I thought I had it lined up, I shot and saw the man flinch. Then I quickly ducked back behind the stairway to reload." In ducking back, Manning missed seeing the outlaw fall from his horse.[139]

His daughter Caroline was only three months old during the bank robbery. Mary, another daughter, was born in 1879. Anselm's wife died shortly after at the age of thirty-six. In 1880, Manning married again, this time to Zilpha Reynolds. Both of his daughters graduated from Carleton College.

Anselm R. Manning, one of the heroes of Northfield, fell dead in the snow from a heart attack while walking to his barn after breakfast on January 6, 1909. He was seventy-five years old. According to Northfield historian Bob Phelps, Manning was "quiet, hard-working, civic-minded, peaceful—but also quick to respond to a crisis, courageous and gritty when necessary, and more than a match for those who threatened him."

William Wallace Murphy

WILLIAM WALLACE MURPHY WAS BORN in Ligonier, Westmorland County, Pennsylvania, on July 27, 1837, of Dutch and Scottish heritage. Upon leaving school in 1854, the sixteen-year-old Murphy went to California seeking his fortune in the gold mines before taking up residency in 1861 in Pittsburgh, Pennsylvania. When the Civil War erupted in 1861, he quickly raised Company G, of the Fourteenth Pennsylvania Regiment, and entered the service as a second lieutenant. He received gunshot wounds in the elbow at Lexington and saber wounds in the head and arm at Piedmont, Virginia, and was promoted to captain of Company D of the same regiment.[140]

Captain Murphy spent the first two years of the war in West Virginia, one of these years under General Philip Henry Sheridan. Taken prisoner at Mimms Flat, he spent three and a half months at Libby Prison and other Confederate prisons. Following General Robert E. Lee's surrender, Captain Murphy's regiment was ordered to Texas, but upon reaching Leavenworth, Kansas, they received news that all Confederate forces in Texas had already surrendered. The regiment was mustered out at Leavenworth. In 1866, Captain Murphy married Inez Atkins and moved to Madelia, where he built a frame house, one of the first south of Mankato, and began to farm and raise stock. He was elected to the state legislature in 1871.

Following the Northfield bank robbery five years later, "Cap" Murphy organized a posse and quickly moved in the direction of

Sheriff Glispin's confrontation with the Youngers in Hanska Slough. En route, they met Mrs. Valentine Schaleben and a neighbor lady who were driving to Madelia and warned them the bandits were nearby and would try and get their horses. The robbers had run into the Watonwan River bottom and taken cover in the "dense wild plum thicket and vines." Trapped in a triangular area, blocked on the south by a cliff, the boys made their last stand. Murphy and company caught up to the Youngers at a point on the north branch of the river where they had concealed themselves in the underbrush. The posse divided into small groups in pursuit of the trapped bandits.[141]

Meanwhile, Glispin asked for volunteers, and seven of the posse advanced upstream following the outlaws. George A. Bradford, one of the seven, was shocked in learning that all sixteen men had not answered the call. Murphy gathered the men together and formed a plan. "Here is the way we'll do it, men," he instructed. "Form a line fifteen feet apart, and we'll walk right at 'em. When we see 'em, demand their surrender, if they shoot, shoot them. Shoot to kill, keep on shooting until they surrender or are all dead, or we are!"[142]

The voice of Captain Murphy broke the silence, and in measured words he said, "Boys this is horrible but you see what lawlessness has brought to you."[143]

Murphy had a surprise waiting for him when he returned to his own wagon. In his haste to chase down the robbers, he had failed to notice his seven-year-old son, Ralph, hiding under a blanket in the bottom of the wagon box. Murphy was shocked that his little boy, from a safe distance, had witnessed the charge of the posse under Sheriff Glispin and himself.[144]

Cole said that just previously to the fight, Captain Murphy had passed five rods away from them while posting men. They decided against killing him, he said, because the gunshot would attract other men to their hiding place. Murphy was thirty-nine years old when he became one of the captors of the Younger brothers at Hanska Slough for which he was praised by several newspapers, including one in Madelia:

"When the Younger brothers were sought on September 21, 1876, Captain Murphy was the spirit of the posse of pursuers. Only through his fearless leadership, it is asserted by persons who best know, the surrender of the bank robbers was accomplished. The Youngers, too, joined in the eulogy to the captain's bravery. When they saw him fording and re-fording the creek, calling his followers from places of safety, the Youngers knew that their most timely act would be to kill him in order to defeat inevitable capture. They fired upon him, one bullet breaking a pipe in his pocket but they did not turn him from his purpose. He advanced upon them, rallying seven brave men from his party. A hand-to-hand fusillade occurred. Pitts was killed, and every member of the band of fugitives was wounded. The fugitives' surrender followed. Then Captain Murphy returned to more peaceful occupations, and had others not told of his heroic generalship, it never would have been known."[145]

Two years later, Captain Murphy found himself on the opposite side of the law when the first of several stories broke in the *Mankato Record*: "Madelia is greatly excited by an extraordinary and distressing incident. On Thursday morning a young man named Samuel Ash, a nephew of Mr. C.D. Ash, of Madelia, exposed his person and made the most disgusting proposals to two little girls, daughters of Mr. Barney Kempher and Captain W.W. Murphy, old and respected citizens. The children ran home and Mr. Kempher went in pursuit of the villain, whom he supposed at the time from the children's account to be a tramp. He found him and Ash admitted the offense and expressed his sorrow. Mr. Kempher placed him in the hands of the sheriff. Captain Murphy hearing his own child's account upon his return from dinner, started off with a gun to shoot the tramp as he supposed. He found him in the sheriff's hands and was talking to him apparently with perfect calmness. Mr. Ash admitted his guilt and said he was sorry for what he had done; didn't know what made him do so, and that he was willing to abide by the law. After some questioning as to what ought to be done with him, Mr. Murphy asked him 'if he didn't know such men ought to be shot.' Someone made the remark to the captain 'that they had better let the law take its course.' When the captain saying he didn't know but they had, raised the gun and asked him, 'How he would like to look into the muzzle of that,' and discharged it, the contents passing through Ash's forearm and into the left side of the chest above the heart. Mr. Ash was just alive Friday morning when our informant left. Captain Murphy has been before the justice on the charge of manslaughter and was remanded on bail."[146]

Ash died the following Monday from the gunshot wounds. Before he passed away, he gave what became his last statement to prosecuting Attorney Daniel Buck, who was accompanied by Justice Charles A. Pomeroy. Pomeroy and Murphy had ironically, been two of the heroes, later dubbed the "Magnificent Seven," who had captured the Youngers in the shootout at Hanska Slough.[147]

Ash said in his dying statement that he had first seen the children—three girls and a boy—walking along the railroad tracks about eleven o'clock on that Thursday morning, and before he caught up to them, they had left the track and climbed over a fence into a pasture. He followed the oldest girl in the party (the daughter of B.O. Kempher), who had parted from the rest of the children towards the far end of the field to pet a colt. Ash allegedly asked her several questions before inquiring "if she ever did anything."

When the girl told him she had not, he offered her fifty cents, which made the other frightened children cry. Ash walked back to the track and called the children to him. They obeyed and were told by Ash to never "let anyone lead them astray." They walked halfway to Madelia with him, but, according to Ash, he never touched any of them, nor did he in any way expose himself.

Ash had given himself up to the sheriff, Kempher, and Murphy in front of J.N. Cheney's office and had made no effort to escape. The defendant, whose parents lived at Beaver Dam, Wisconsin, said he had met the children outside Riverdale where he worked for a man named W. Bradford. Ash said when Murphy shot him, the muzzle was only two inches from his breast. He said he was certain that Captain Murphy had shot him intentionally.

Ash's account of his behavior was supported by the testimony of the children, who maintained that he never spoke or acted improperly towards Murphy's daughter. According to the *Mankato Review*, "this fact, and Ash's youth, he is about [nineteen] or [twenty] years old, have tended to produce a good deal of strong feeling in Madelia against Murphy for having, as is thought, purposely killed Ash without any sufficient excuse."[148]

Captain Murphy maintained that the gun went off accidentally, but the sheriff stated that both locks had previously been on half-cock. The charge of shot passed through the left lung near the heart and broke the shoulder blade. Murphy's bail, set at $800, was paid, and he returned home. On Monday night, however, when it was learned that Ash had died, Murphy was arrested again. An examination between Justice Buck, the prosecutor, and M.J. Severance for the defense was held on Wednesday and Thursday. After hearing the argument on both sides, the justice committed Murphy for trial at the next term of District Court, refusing to grant bail, and on Friday morning, the defendant was turned over to the sheriff of Blue Earth County, and placed in jail.

The trial of Captain Murphy for the killing of young Ash commenced on December 20, 1878, at St. James. Once a jury was selected, the case was recapitulated by Attorney General Wilson for the State and Ex-Governor Cushman K. Davis for the defense. At 11:30 A.M., the jury asked for further instruction by asking Judge Dickinson, "Are we confined to conviction or acquittal for murder in the second degree, as charged in the indictment?"[149]

Judge Dickinson told them they could convict of a lesser degree. Warren Case then asked for the definition of murder in the third degree, which the judge clarified. M.K. Armstrong then asked for the definition of the third and fourth degrees of manslaughter. After the judge defined these points, William Melick told the court they had no additional questions. J. Hopkins, however, inquired whether it was necessary to bring in a verdict if the incident was considered an accidental shooting. The judge replied that a verdict of not guilty would be proper in that case.

While the jury met through the night, Judge Dickinson returned to court, but was told that the jurors were unable to reach a verdict. The judge told them they would have to remain until a verdict was agreed upon, for another jury would face the same problems. The jurors were permitted to go for a walk with the sheriff but otherwise had to remain in the room where they were meeting.

Soon after dinner, Judge Dickinson was informed that the jury had reached a verdict. Judge, jury, prisoner, and about forty other persons met in the courtroom where Captain Murphy was found guilty of manslaughter in the fourth degree. The defendant became livid when the sentence was pronounced but seemed greatly relieved when he was released on $7,000 bail.

On February 8, 1879, the *Mankato Record* announced that Captain Murphy would be returning to court in St. James on February 12th.[150] During the hearing, the counsel for the defendant filed a bill of exceptions to the verdict and moved for a new trial, which motion was denied. The court then passed sentence, imposing a fine of $600, and in default the prisoner to be committed to the Blue Earth County Jail for one year or until the fine was paid. A notice of appeal was served, and the amount of the recognizance set at $2,000.[151]

Captain Murphy was brought to Madelia on November 13th to begin serving his one-year sentence in the Blue Earth County Jail. Rather than pay the $600 fine, he chose to spend the year in jail, even though some of his relatives had agreed to pay the fine. "We think Captain Murphy has exhibited bad taste," proclaimed the *Mankato Free Press*. "He had better sold his old boots rather than do what he has done."[152]

Captain Murphy died in at his home near Madelia on Friday, August 19, 1904, of heart complications at the age sixty-five. His funeral was held in the home two days later and conducted by the Masonic Lodge. The body was laid to rest in the Madelia Cemetery. He was survived by his wife and seven children, Mrs. Murphy passing on in 1927.[153]

Charles A. Pomeroy

CHARLES A. POMEROY WAS BORN IN RUTLEDGE, Cattaraugus County, New York. He came to Madelia in 1855 with his father, who was one of the area's earliest settlers, when Minnesota was still a territory. Pomeroy became a justice of the peace and witnessed the Great Sioux Uprising in 1862. He was described as "short, compact, powerfully built, quiet in disposition, industrious, and unobtrusive, yet cool and courageous in danger."

Pomeroy did not hear of the proximity of the robbers on that memorable 21st of September until the first squad of Madelia men had started for the scene, but the moment the news reached his ears, he armed himself, mounted his horse and headed after them, reaching the field to offer himself as one of the seven volunteers who undertook the perilous attack.

He married in 1879 and remained in Madelia through the turn of the century. He died in Valley City, North Dakota, in 1941.

Minnesota Grit

General Edmund Mann Pope

CIVIL WAR HERO, GENERAL E.M. POPE, was born in Pennfield, New York, on February 21, 1837. On July 22, 1861, the day after the Bull Run disaster, a tidal wave of patriotism rolled over the entire North from the Atlantic to the Pacific coast, leaving its impression on every loyal heart, and a deep-seated feeling that the Rebellion must be put down and the Union preserved intact, regardless of cost, of treasure, and of precious lives. On that day two members of Company F, Fifty-fourth Regiment, New York State Militia (Rochester City Dragoons), met on the street in Rochester, and, as a matter of course, conversation turned on the subject that was uppermost in all minds. Both expressing the intention of adding their mite by offering their services, and lives if necessary, in the preservation of the Union, one suggested the feasibility of recruiting a regiment of cavalry. They parted to meet the next day, and after a few meetings and discussions the two men went to Albany to interview Governor Morgan. They received authority from him to raise a regiment of cavalry to serve three years, or during the war. They returned to Rochester and immediately opened a recruiting office. They secured the county fairgrounds and buildings for barracks and camps.[154]

On November 14, 1861, Colonel Samuel J. Crooks received authority to recruit the Eighth New York Cavalry Regiment at

Rochester for three years' service. Ten companies were organized, drilled and mustered into the United States service November 23, 1861. November 28th, the regiment left Rochester for Washington, where it remained as part of the force in defense of the Capital until March 9, 1862.

During this time rumors were rife that the military authorities thought they were getting more cavalry than was needed, and that a number of regiments which had not been mounted would be disbanded or reorganized as infantry. Colonel Crooks having resigned, the officers arrived at the conclusion that, if some cavalry officer of the regular army—of well-known ability—were appointed to the command of the regiment, it would enhance the prospect of their retention and being mounted. They unanimously joined in a request to General Stoneman, then in command of the cavalry, to recommend some tried officer of this description for the colonelcy, setting forth the fact that the regiment was composed of a superior body of men, and if fully equipped and commanded by an officer of well-known skill, it would be a credit to the army and render efficient service to the country. He commended their course and complied with the request. The wisdom of this action on the part of the officers was fully demonstrated afterwards by the glorious career of the regiment.

The regiment broke camp at Washington on March 9, 1862, and was placed on guard along the upper Potomac and canal from Edwards Ferry to Point of Rocks. On April 6th, it was ordered to Harper's Ferry, where they guarded the railroad from that point to Winchester until May 24th, the time of Nathaniel Banks' retreat before Jackson, when the regiment fell back to Harper's Ferry. In anticipation of an attack on this place, the men volunteered for this occasion to take muskets and help defend the place. They were furnished with muskets and forty rounds of ammunition, and in this shape marched up to Bolivar Heights and took position on the extreme right of the line of battle there formed, and were the last recalled when the line was withdrawn the same night.

The men were posted on Maryland Heights where they were engaged in picket duty until about the 23d of June, when they were ordered to Relay House, near Baltimore, for the purpose of being mounted and fully equipped. Here they were joined by Capt. B.F. Davis, of the First U.S. Cavalry, who had been commissioned as colonel of the Eighth New York Cavalry at the request of the officers of the regiment, upon the recommendation of General Stoneman. The regiment remained at Relay House, the men drilling assiduously until the early part of September, when they were ordered to Harper's Ferry, from which point they were daily reconnoitering up to the night of the 14th of September, when they accomplished their ever memorable escape from that place.

Harper's Ferry at this time being completely invested on all sides and it being a foregone conclusion that the place would surrender, Colonel Davis received the reluctant consent of Colonel Miles, who was in command, to make the attempt at saving the cavalry by withdrawing them and forcing their way through enemy lines. Soon after dark on the night of September 14, the Eighth New York Cavalry, the Twelfth Illinois Cavalry, and a portion of the First Maryland Cavalry, all under command of Colonel Davis, crossed the pontoon bridge to the Maryland side of the Potomac and commenced their perilous night march. A little before daylight on the morning of the 15th, they captured Longstreet's ammunition train on the Hagerstown Pike, about three miles from Williamsport, which they turned and hurried along at breakneck speed for Greencastle, Pennsylvania, reaching there about the middle of the forenoon. Then, proceeding more leisurely, the train, consisting of some seventy-five to eighty wagons and some 300 horses and mules, moved on to Chambersburg. The brigade rested at Greencastle that night. The next day they joined McClellan on the battlefield of Antietam. Colonel Davis was brevetted major, U.S.A., on the recommendation of General McClellan, for conspicuous conduct in the management of the withdrawal of the cavalry from Harper's Ferry at the surrender of that place.

About the 1st of October, the regiment took the advance along with other cavalry in pursuit of the Confederate army, which was falling back to the Rappahannock River, by the way of the Shenandoah Valley, and the turnpike leading south on the west side of the Blue Ridge Mountains. After crossing the Potomac River at Berlin, the first engagement in which the regiment participated was at Snickersville, on the 27th day of October 1862, when it dashed boldly up the Pike leading through the Gap. It had barely covered a quarter of the distance to the Gap when a concealed battery opened on them with canister and compelled them to fall back, which they did in good order.

Then in rapid succession followed the engagements at Philomont, Unionville, Upperville, Barbee's Cross Roads, Sulphur Springs, Amissville, Corbin's Cross Roads, and Jefferson. Those of Philomont, Unionville, Upperville, Amissville, and Jefferson were sharp skirmishes in which the regiment lost quite largely in men killed and wounded, while that at Barbee's Cross Roads was a savage one while it lasted and first gave the regiment that confidence in itself which it afterwards maintained to the close of the war. It was the first fair charge of cavalry against cavalry of any magnitude in which it had engaged, and the enemy was completely routed. On this field the writer saw for the first time the corpse of a cavalryman, killed with a sabre.

A part of the regiment was dismounted and sent ahead to skirmish and dislodge a portion of the Rebels who were also fighting dismounted and endeavoring to hold our advance in check. While our dismounted men were skirmishing behind a stone wall, Colonel Davis led the remainder over a small knoll and formed them in a hollow, out of sight of the enemy. They were but just formed when a large regiment of Rebel cavalry came charging down upon them. Before the Rebels had reached the brow of the knoll the command, "Charge!" was given, and in a moment that mounted part of the regiment charged so unexpectedly and so impetuously that the enemy broke and fled in the wildest disorder, leaving many of their number in our hands, dead, wounded, or prisoners. An extract from General McClellan's report of this engagement reads: "A largely superior force charged Colonel Davis' Eighth New York Cavalry, but were gallantly met and repulsed."

At Jefferson, the regiment participated in its last engagement for the year 1862. The weather was growing quite cold, and the men were not as yet furnished with shelter tents. They were obliged to lie out all night on the damp ground, and nearly all the time were denied the privilege of fire. Their sufferings were not inconsiderable. But they were made happy by being ordered into regular camp at Belle Plain, from where they were sent at intervals to do picket duty on the Rappahannock River, which formed the dividing line between the two armies.

At an early date in 1863, active operations again began on the part of the regiment, which had been strengthened by the addition of three new companies, recruited at Rochester by Major William H. Benjamin during August, September, and October, 1862, he having been detailed from the regiment for this duty. Up to June 9, 1863, the day of the cavalry fight at Beverly Ford, the Eighth Cavalry had participated in fourteen different engagements of more or less importance, losing in killed, wounded, and missing, about fifty men, the greater part of the losses occurring at Independence Hill, March 4th, and Freeman's Ford, April 15th. At the time of the battle of Chancellorsville they were engaged several days in operations around the right flank of their own and the left flank of the Confederates, coming inside of their line over the breastworks on the extreme right a little before sunset May 4th, and that night fell back with the main body of the army.

The great cavalry battle at Beverly Ford, June 9, 1863, deserves special mention. In this battle the regiment took the leading part, and lost more men in killed and wounded than any other regiment engaged. Before it was fairly light they dashed across the Ford and into the very midst of the Rebel camps. During the whole fight the Eighth was in the thickest of it, winning much glory, but at the expense of many gallant officers and men. It was here, and in the first dash, that the gallant Colonel Davis fell mortally wounded at the head of his regiment. His loss was deeply deplored, not by his own regiment alone, but by the entire cavalry corps. Lieutenant Colonel William L. Markell was promoted to the vacancy, and became colonel of the regiment. From Beverly Ford to Gettysburg the regiment was marching and skirmishing almost daily.

Late in the afternoon of June 30th, the regiment, leading the advance of the First Brigade, First Division, Cavalry Corps, entered Gettysburg, passed through the town, and bivouacked near the Seminary in an open field on the left of the Cashtown Pike, from which one squadron advancing about a mile established a picket line across and on both sides of the Cashtown Road. About seven o'clock on the next morning, July 1st, the officer commanding the squadron on picket gave notice that the enemy in strong force was advancing on his pickets from the direction of Cashtown. The brigade was formed in line of battle as soon as possible about a mile in front of the Seminary, and three squadrons deployed as skirmishers were advanced to the support of the picket line now being driven back by the enemy.

The fighting soon became general and sharp along the whole line, the Union skirmishers stubbornly resisting every inch of the enemy's advance although the Confederates were there in overpowering numbers. In a short time the line was compelled to fall back to the next ridge, less than a quarter of a mile in the rear. The skirmishers fighting stubbornly in the meantime behind fences and trees, and federal artillery providing good execution, the advance of the enemy was retarded, and this line was maintained until about ten o'clock, when the First Corps, the advance of federal infantry, came up and relieved the Cavalry Brigade in its unequal contest with the enemy. Considering that two divisions of Hill's Corps were held in check for three hours by so small a cavalry force, it becomes unnecessary to say anything more about their gallantry and fighting qualities. The regimental monument of the Eighth New York now stands on the spot the regiment occupied when relieved by the First Corps, on what is now known as Reynolds Avenue, and a few rods in rear of the spot where General Reynolds was killed.

In the afternoon the enemy, being strongly reinforced, extended his flanks, and made a desperate attempt to turn the federal left. They advanced in three strong lines, when Pope's brigade was ordered forward at a trot and deployed. Half of the command was dismounted and placed behind a portion of a stone wall on a ridge of woods, with the Seminary on their right. The enemy being close upon them, they opened an effective, rapid fire with breechloading carbines, which killed and wounded many of the Confederate first line, that after a short heroic struggle to continue the advance, they could stand it no longer and fell back on the second line. Pope's men kept up the fire until the enemy, in overwhelming numbers, approached so near that in order to save their men and horses, the federals mounted and fell back rapidly to the next ridge, carrying their wounded with them. The stand they made against the enemy prevented their left flank from being turned, and saved a division of federal infantry.

After Gettysburg, while Lee was falling back towards Richmond, their experience was a repetition of that after the Antietam battle, except that the engagements were more frequent and severe. Hanging on to Lee's flank, watching every opportunity to harass and punish his retreating troops, they were marching and fighting almost daily. From Gettysburg, until the last of November, when the active campaign was closed and camp established near Culpepper, the regiment participated in twenty-six different engagements, some of which were mere skirmishes and others were quite severe cavalry fights, losing in killed, wounded, and missing over 150 men. On February 27, 1864, Colonel Markell resigned, and

Lieutenant-Colonel William H. Benjamin succeeded to the command. In due time he was commissioned colonel.

From the beginning of the year 1864, to the time of the battles of the Wilderness, the regiment took part in only two engagements. Pope took time off and married Mary B. Frisbie in 1864 while home on furlough from the war. From that time on the predictions of a lively campaign were verified, and a day passed without a fight of more or less severity was the exception; the regiment distinguished itself by many gallant acts. During March 1864, the regiment which had up to that time been in the First Division, Cavalry Corps, A.P., became a part of the Second Brigade of the Third Division. The regiment accompanied Sheridan on the great raid at Richmond, and took an active part in nearly every engagement. After the raid, it was in three quite severe engagements, in one of which, at Hawes Shop, Colonel Benjamin, while gallantly leading the regiment, was wounded.

The Eighth went to Petersburg, and did picket duty in the vicinity of Prince George Court House until the date of General Wilson's raid. Accompanying the raid the regiment lost heavily— on June 22nd—cutting their way through the Rebel right at Reams' Station, on the 23d, at Black and Whites, to near Nottoway Court House, where the brigade, being cut off from the main command, had an afternoon and all night battle, sustaining a loss of ninety men.

On the 24th, it succeeded in joining the command at Meherrin Station, on the Dansville Railroad; on the 25th, to Roanoke Creek; and at night, to Staunton River; 27th, to Meherrin River; 28th, to Stony Creek Station, on the Weldon Railroad, in rear of the Rebel lines, where all afternoon and night they were trying to cut their way through, but were again headed off by the enemy and forced to make their way back south nearly to the North Carolina line. After enduring untold hardships, they at last found their way into the Union lines, the regiment losing nearly one-third of its number.

August 8th, the regiment was shipped to Washington and proceeded to Winchester, in the Shenandoah Valley, where they were prominent in all the gallant engagements under Sheridan, in which the Eighth won special mention from both the division and corps commanders.

On October 29th, the expiration of its term of enlistment, those entitled were ordered to Rochester to be discharged and mustered out. Many of the men and officers re-enlisted, and together with those whose term had not expired were consolidated into a battalion of eight companies and retained in the service. April 30, 1865, four new companies were formed of recruits mustered in for one and two years, and the regimental organization was again completed. Lieutenant Colonel Edmund M. Pope, original captain of Company A, was commissioned colonel, February 14th, and he ably commanded the regiment until the close of the war.

On the 27th of February 1865, the regiment was on the march southward from Winchester, and on March second, encountering the enemy in force at Waynesborough under General Jubal Early, a sharp battle ensued, resulting in a signal victory for our side, leaving in our hands about 1,500 prisoners, five pieces of artillery, and ten battle flags. Major Compson, who commanded the regiment in this engagement, was awarded a Medal of Honor for the capture of a battle flag. The Waynesborough affair over, the march to Petersburg was continued, and the command took a prominent part in the last and effective campaign of the war.

This regiment received the flag of truce sent in by General Lee at Appomattox, June 9, 1865. The regiment, commanded by Colonel M. Pope, was mustered out and honorably discharged June 27, 1865, at Alexandria, Virginia. Eight officers and sixty enlisted men were killed in action; five officers and thirty-two enlisted men died of wounds received in action; six officers and 213 enlisted men died of disease and other causes: total, nineteen officers, 305 enlisted men; aggregate, 324, of whom three officers and seventy enlisted men died in the hands of the enemy.[155]

Following the Civil War, Pope organized a cavalry force on the Rio Grande with Generals Merritt and Custer before a peaceful solution to the troubles with Mexico was reached. At the time of the Northfield bank robbery, he was living in Mankato as a dealer in farm produce and machinery.[156]

When news of the Northfield raid reached Mankato, Pope was placed in charge of several posses and coordinated a constant pursuit of the robbers. Already telegrams had been sent to nearly every town and hamlet in the state of Minnesota when General Pope, the famed Civil War hero, was called in to coordinate the search efforts. Assuming command, he quickly declared, "We'll soon get them."

According to a Mankato newspaper, General Pope's impeccable war record made him the right man for the job: "General Pope's war record is a particularly brilliant one. There were few harder fighters or more determined campaigners than he. Not knowing the meaning of fear, he never shirked a duty, no matter how arduous, and chose the most dangerous assignments."[157]

Meanwhile, the Winona Railroad Company ordered that an engine at Mankato be prepared to patrol the track between Mankato and Janesville. Placed at the disposal of General Pope, who was headquartering at Eagle Lake, the train continually hauled troops from one post to another. An evening train was sent to convey bread, sausages, cheese, and other foods to Pope's train because of the "unreasonable charge made for meals to hunters."[158]

Following the capture, he returned to his farm produce and machinery business on Front Street in Mankato. Pope held several offices, including a term as state senator and is regarded the father of the movement for the establishment of the State Soldiers' Home. He is also called the father of the Mankato Public Library where he served as board president for many years. When John Lind was elected governor of Minnesota, he selected General Pope as public examiner. Pope died of heart failure in Grand Marais, Minnesota, in June 1906 after delivering a Memorial Day address.[159]

Benjamin A. Rice

BENJAMIN A. RICE WAS THE SON OF W.D. RICE, a prominent judge and senator from St. James. Born in Green County, Alabama, February 8, 1851, he moved with his parents to Arkansas the following year. Benjamin was educated at Christian Brothers College in St. Louis before moving with his family to Minnesota in 1869, settling in St. James the following year. The town was not then surveyed. In 1873, at the age of twenty-two, he was appointed engrossing clerk in the state legislature, in which his father repeatedly served as member.

Young Rice was noted for both the ardent, impetuous temperament and chivalrous manners of a Southern gentleman. He was exceptionally expert in the use of arms, being, for quickness and accuracy of aim, the equal of any of the robbers he encountered at the Watonwan River. He was one of two men from St. James that the reappearance of the Youngers drew to the scene—G.S. Thompson being the other.

Only twenty-five years old the day the Youngers were captured, the expert shootist Rice was said to be by a comrade who marched to his side, "the coolest in combat," and completely in his element.

In the autumn of 1877, Rice moved to Murfreesboro, Tennessee, and married Sallie Bell Wright. He later moved to Lake Weir, Florida where he died August 14, 1889, leaving a widow and two children.

S.J. "Slim" Severson

S.J. "SLIM" SEVERSON, BORN IN WISCONSIN of Norwegian parents in 1855, was the only one of the seven captors of that nationality. Coming to Minnesota, he spent several years working on a farm in the Kenyon area before taking a job as a clerk in a Madelia clothing store where he was employed at the time of the raid.

A friend, who knew the twenty-one-year-old Severson during his confrontation with the robbers, said of him: "The jolliest and most popular young man, especially among his customers. He spoke several languages well. To his wit and good nature, everybody will bear witness, especially the ladies. He is a good salesman, industrious, correct, and to be depended on. He is short, stout and a little 'daredevil' if any trouble is on hand."

Mr. Severson quickly caught the news of the discovery of the robbers and was among the first to join in the chase and subsequent assault. He fired upon the Youngers from the open ground, following them through the slough, and hunting them in their hiding place. Like Mr. Bradford, he was slightly wounded in the wrist by the first shot fired by the gang—a mere graze of the skin—but enough to remind him that they were not shooting into the air.

He moved to Brookings, South Dakota, following his heroism at Hanska Slough, and passed away in Milbank in 1895.

Asle Oscar Sorbel

ASLE OSCAR SORBEL, WHOSE GALLANT RIDE led to the capture of the Younger brothers, was born on March 9, 1859, in Brown County, Minnesota. He spent the first twenty-four years of his life in the state.

Two weeks after the Northfield raid, the outlaws were walking down a road along Lake Linden in Brown County. Passing a farm, they nodded at a boy milking cows. The boy was this same Asle Oscar Sorbel. Recalled Sorbel: "It was the 21st of September, just two weeks after the raid. Mind you, it had been a steady drizzling rain for two weeks, and it was early morning. The sun was up about twenty minutes. We had the cattle in the road as it was too muddy in the pen. Jim Younger and Charley (sic) Pitts came walking, and they walked one on each side of Pa. He was milking. I had come up to the gate, and as they were far enough so they did not hear me, I said to Pa, 'That was the robbers.' 'No,' he said, 'they was nice men.'"[160]

Oscar's father, Ole, was impressed by the way the two men had given him a friendly, "Good morning," the pair all the while stroking the back of one of the cows in the road. When the strangers passed out of sight, young Sorbel stepped into the mud in the road and examined their toe prints. He found their boots to be very worn.[161]

"I walked over to the road and their big toes showed in the mud," continued Sorbel. "I said, 'Come here. I will show you how nice men they are.' [Pa] said, 'You never mind. Go and milk.' I milked one cow and then I set the pail inside the fence and started after them. There was a bend in the road and timber, so I did not see them, but they crossed the creek about eighty rods west. I could see where they had gone into the timber. I went to three neighbors and told them."[162]

Young Sorbel later stated: "Father hallowed to me and said if it was the robbers they would shoot me. When they were out of sight I went to Mads Owen's, and asked if he had [seen] some men passing. He said he hadn't. I looked in the road to see if there were any tracks, but couldn't see any. Went to Gilbert Christensen's house. Went upon the roof of Christensen's house and looked all around but didn't see them. Then got down and went upon a high hill, looked all around and couldn't see anything. It was early in the morning and no folks [were] out."[163]

The three neighbors to whom Sorbel spread the alarm were Anton Ouren, Mads Ouren, and Gutterson Grove. Unable to locate the fugitives, Sorbel ran up a hill east of the Grove farm and studied the three roads to New Ulm, Madelia, and Lockstock but, again, could not locate the robbers. Returning to the Anton Owen farm, he instructed Anton Anderson, Jens Nilsson, and Armund Brustingen to run up the hill and watch the roads. Sorbel said he was going to ride to Madelia for help.[164]

While young Oscar was following the outlaw trail, a second pair of robbers returned to the Sorbel farm and turned in at the old log house where Guri Sorbel was busy preparing breakfast for her family. Immediately, she noticed that one of the men was limping and leaning on his pal. In greeting her, they asked if they could buy some food, telling her they had baked some bread the day before, but it had soured on them. One of the men put down some money from a roll of bills.[165]

The men informed Mrs. Sorbel that they were hunters and were very hungry. They asked for breakfast and were told the meal wasn't ready but that they were welcome to wait while she cooked it. The two men said they could not wait. Taking some bread and butter, they thanked her and disappeared into the timber.[166]

When Oscar reached home, he was informed that two more men had stopped at the farm. "I wanted to go to Ouren's and tell them there were four," remembered Oscar. Father wouldn't let me—said they might shoot me. I sent one of my sisters over. Asked for a horse to go to town but he wouldn't let me have it. Then father said if I would go to the east road so they could not see me, he would let me have one. The horses were on the wagon, [I] unhitched them, took harness off, took one and went through our fields and through one of Torre Olson's, hollered to his folks that the robbers were around, went on to town. Ran him all I could."[167]

Before his ride, Oscar had told his sisters to tell the neighbors there were four men rather than two. She was then to go to the big hill and watch the road with the others. Oscar mounted a horse and dashed seven miles into Madelia to report the news.[168]

On the way, he kept to the timber side of the lake so the robbers could not see him. "About two miles from Madelia, my horse fell flat in the mud, and I, too," remembered Sorbel. "Well, I jumped on again, and when I got to Madelia, I was all mud from head to foot. The first man I met did not believe me and asked who knew me. I told them I knew John Owen, and they went after him, and he said he would stand good for that I spoke the truth."[169]

Galloping down the street, he headed straight to the Flanders Hotel and Colonel Vought, who had first told him of the robbers' presence in the area. "Went first to Vought's hotel and hollered that robbers were around, and if you want to make money, got to hurry up," recalled Sorbel.[170]

Vought ran to Sheriff James Glispin, and a small posse of men was formed. The first five men to leave Madelia and arrive at the Sorbel farm were Sheriff Glispin, Colonel Thomas L. Vought, Dr. George H. Overholt, W.R. Estes, and S.J. Severson. Soon Charles Pomeroy, Jr., George A. Bradford, and Captain W.W. Murphy joined them. Two men from St. James—Benjamin Rice and G.S. Thompson—also met them at the scene.[171] From these ten would emerge the Magnificent Seven, consisting of Glispin, Vought, Captain W.W. Murphy, George Bradford, Charles Pomeroy, Jr., Benjamin Rice, and Ole Severson. Word spread quickly throughout the county, and soon, scores of other men were grabbing guns and horses and joining the chase.[172]

"Men started up, and I lent horse to a man to go after the robbers and rode back home in a wagon," recollected Sorbel. "The man could hardly get him back. The horse was so fat you could hardly feel his ribs, and I rode him too fast going to town. The distance by road is eight to ten miles, and rode it in an hour. The roads were very bad."[173]

Meanwhile, the robbers had started southwest from the area of the Sorbel farm looking for horses. It was rumored that on the way to Northfield, they had visited the Doolittle horse ranch outside Madelia, and it was a good bet the boys remembered the ranch and were trying to get back there. But the Doolittles remembered too and had taken their fine horses northwest toward Comfrey.[174]

"When we got back to the place where the robbers were, the men were going into the brush," recalled Sorbel. "I wanted to go in and took hold of a Yankee's gun; he told me to mind my business, and hold the horses. Would have gone into the bush if I had a gun."[175]

The robbers stopped first at the farm of a man named Andrew Anderson. The farmer, who was aware of the robbers' quest for horses in the area, quickly turned his mounts loose in seeing the men approach. The robbers then met two mounted hunters from the Twin Cities, but the men, very suspicious, fled on horseback.[176]

Sorbel reached the Anderson house just in time to see the robbers' departing. He was told by a lawman that had also just arrived, that he would get a reward even though he would not be in on the capture. Sorbel said he needed the money to go to school and inquired whether he would receive the money before he was of age, as he did not care for all of it just then.[177]

But the posses were closing in. Sorbel's band of farmers, back near the farm, were still watching from the hill. "When the boys got on the hill, the robbers were half a mile southeast heading for St. James," recalled Suborn. "The boys sent [a] man on horseback, telling us where to go. One of the [outlaw] boys went ahead on horseback to three threshing machines and had them unhitch their horses and strike for the prairie."[178]

From three-quarters of a mile away, Sorbel's neighbors could see the robbers riding stolen horses from the threshers towards the prairie. Said Sorbel later: "They had three horses on the prairie, but their hobbles were locked, and so they could not get them off for about four miles. North of town we met Einor Smisma, who told us to go west, as the robbers were heading southwest and after that, we met several men who told us where to go. So we got to the timber about seven miles from St. James, just as the robbers got there."[179]

Oscar Sorbel remembered how badly the Younger boys had been shot up: "Cole Younger had one bullet and some buckshot received at Northfield, besides ten fresh buckshot in his body, but he did not pray. He offered to fight two of our best men at once. He said he had been dogged for two weeks in the rain, with nothing to eat, but that he could lick two of our best men. Bob slung his left arm around him and said, 'Come, or we will be hanged.' But Cole said he did not care, and that he would just as soon hang today as tomorrow."[180]

As the badly wounded Youngers were helped out of Hanska Slough, they watched as the body of Charlie Pitts was being carried toward a waiting wagon. Bob Younger asked for a chew of tobacco, and some of the posse men said he should not be given any. But young Sorbel was there: "I went over to Oke Wisty and got a ten-cent plug and handed it to Bob who took about half of it in one chew, and was going to hand it back. But I told him to keep it."[181]

Two days later, Sorbel met the captured Youngers again, and this time, he was recognized by them as being the same young man who had spread the alarm which had led to their capture. Recalled Sorbel: "Bob said, 'Why, that is the boy who gave me the tobacco.' Cole made quite a speech to me, saying I did my duty, but if they had suspected me, they would either have shot me, or taken me along."

Sorbel would later talk with them again at Stillwater Prison on two occasions, and Cole informed him that it was he and Bob who came to his father's house looking for food during their first meeting. He also confessed that during the visit to the farm, Bob had concealed his wounded arm in a sling beneath his coat. Cole said he and his brother never suspected that the boy's father knew they were the robbers who were then being hunted.

Oscar's mother Guri sent flowers to the Youngers after they were incarcerated in Madelia. She obtained special permission to visit Bob at the Flanders and pleaded to him for forgiveness. Bob, moved by her emotions, replied, "I have nothing to blame you for, madame."[182]

Oscar's father, Ole Suborn, was killed early in 1879 while returning from New Ulm. His team ran off a bridge about two feet high, the wagon fell upon him, breaking his neck.[183]

In 1883, afraid of retribution from members of the James-Younger Gang, Oscar moved to the Dakota Territory, and settled on a farm in Nutley Township, Day County. On July 11, 1890, Sorbel married Minnie Westgard, and the couple moved to Webster four years later, Oscar working as a veterinarian.

"My dad when I was young used horse and buggy or sled and went to the country for a week at a time," recalled Oscar's son, A. R. Sorbel. "He carried a twist. It is like a billy club with a small rope on the end of it. Used to twist around the nose of a horse when doing, extracting, or leveling the longer teeth. He carried a .32 caliber revolver and had a wolfhound with him."[184]

Oscar Sorbel was seventy-one years old when he passed away on July 11, 1930, coincidentally on the fortieth anniversary of his marriage. In addition to Minnie, he left behind seven children, three sisters, a brother, and eleven grandchildren.[185]

Elias Stacy

ONE CITIZEN, ELIAS STACY, ARMED WITH a loaded shotgun, rushed to the corner where Clell Miller was remounting his horse during the Northfield fracas.[186] Miller was directly in front of the bank, and as the outlaw turned to face him, Stacy surprised him with a full load of birdshot in the face. Miller was knocked from his horse but was not injured seriously, and Stacy ran for cover.

The three Stacy brothers—Elias, Julius, and Albert moved to Franklyn, Quebec, Canada, shortly after the Northfield raid. Albert, age thirty-two, died shortly thereafter on October 17, 1877, in Franklyn.[187] Elias Stacy passed away in Franklyn, Quebec, in March 1882.[188]

Thomas Lent Vought

THOMAS LENT VOUGHT, BORN IN WOLCOTT, New York, April 29, 1833, Thomas Vought was forty-three years old at the time of the capture. At the age of nineteen, Vought moved to La Crosse, Wisconsin and married Hester Green. Living in Bryce Prairie when the Civil War broke out, he served with the Fourteenth Wisconsin Regiment for the entire campaign. In 1866, he journeyed to Madelia where he began farming and stock raising and opened a stagecoach line. When the railroad appropriated his business, he purchased the Flanders House.

About August 23, 1876, two men stopped at the Flanders House and registered as J.C. King and Jack Ward. They arrived in the middle of the afternoon on two beautiful horses. The men wore broad hats, large gold watches and heavy fobs, and displayed plenty of money. They conveyed to Colonel Vought that they were making a preliminary survey for the railroad and seemed to be quite interested in the road west and north of Madelia.

Following the robbery two weeks later, Thomas L. Vought, began putting two and two together. He recalled the two men who had stopped at his hotel a couple weeks earlier, purporting to be cattle buyers. They had certainly asked more than their share of questions about the lay of the land. With a friend, Vought started off for the country north and west of Madelia.[189]

The two men went to a growth of trees near a bridge that Vought remembered telling the "cattle buyers" about. Vought was sure the strangers would come out of the woods at the bridge, and he and his companion concealed themselves in the underbrush to await the passing of the fugitives. While concealed in the bushes, the two men were discovered by a young man of "about sixteen" who was herding cattle. The inquisitive boy, Asle Oscar Sorbel, refused to leave until they told him why they were in hiding and for whom they were waiting. When told they were waiting for the Northfield bank robbers, the boy's curiosity was satisfied. Before he left them, he commented, "Gee! I'd love to take a shot at those fellows with dad's old gun."[190]

"My oldest brother was driving Horace Thompson, then president of the First National Bank of St. Paul, his wife and niece, who were vacationing and hunting," recalled T.L. Vought. "They were on the prairie, while the robbers were down on the Watonwan River bottoms in a thicket of willows and plum brush, and it is presumed the robbers thought they would get out and get the horses and try to escape if possible."[191]

Other accounts stated that Thompson and his sons were hunting prairie chickens when they came upon some robbers. The outlaws planned to steal their horses from a wagon, but in confusing Thompson's shotgun for a rifle, they disappeared into the thicket, thinking they were part of the posse.[192]

With rapid firing continuing from both sides, two of the posse men were hit in the exchange, although their wounds were not serious. Colonel Vought doubled up from a bullet, which had struck him just above the waist. Clutching his lower vest pocket, Vought was surprised to find the bullet had shattered a large rosewood pipe he carried. The bullet itself was found in his cartridge belt.[193]

The three outlaw brothers were taken up the hill. A lumber wagon pulled by a team of horses was driven into the bushes, and after Pitts' body was dumped in the bottom, the Youngers were placed on spring seats. Cole was greeted by Colonel Vought, who remembered him as the man who had registered at the Flanders Hotel under the name of J.C. King.

Vought later recalled, "He recognized me and held out his blood-covered hand and shook my hand and called me landlord. Allow me to mention a little scene, which made a deep impression on my mind. The bold desperadoes, horribly mangled, were under the care of seven well-armed men who stood over them wearing sad faces. For a short time all was silent save the rustling of the leaves in the underbrush."[194]

The dead robber (Pitts) was described as being six-feet tall, 175 pounds, dark, thick black hair with heavy moustache and goatee. The fatal wound had entered his left breast, one-inch from the center of the breastbone and approximately three inches from the neck. He had also been wounded in the right hip. Mrs. Vought provided clean sheets for the body as well as clean underclothing and shirts for the Youngers.

Cole remembered Colonel Vought from several weeks earlier, and although badly wounded, pointed out the room he had occupied at the time."

Following the capture, the Voughts lived in New York, Elkton, South Dakota (where he was in the hotel business), and Wisconsin. He passed away in LaCrosse, Wisconsin, in August 1917 leaving seven children.

John Koblas

Dr. Henry Mason Wheeler

DR. HENRY MASON WHEELER WAS BORN IN New Hampshire on June 23, 1854, and moved at the age of two with his family to Minnesota where his father opened a pharmacy on Northfield's Division Street. Wheeler graduated from Carleton College in 1875, and for a short time, apprenticed himself to a local farmer, C.W. Thompson. He entered medical school at the University of Michigan that same year and was a student at the time of the Northfield raid.[195]

Henry M. Wheeler, who had been sitting in front of his father's drugstore on the east side of the street when the Northfield raid commenced, had grown suspicious. He had witnessed General Adelbert Ames with his daughter leave the bank and walk toward the mill. After seeing three strangers go into the bank and two more in front of the building, he walked down to the bank. When he saw Allen struggling with Miller, he began shouting, "Robbery! Robbery!"[196]

Wheeler reacted quickly. "While I was sitting reading, I noticed three men tying their horses on the opposite side of the street, and after consulting together, they went into the bank," he remembered. "Their actions seemed peculiar, and I got up and stepped into the street, when two more horsemen, whom I afterwards learned were Clell Miller and Cole Younger, rode up from the south and also dismounted.

"Miller was the nearest to the bank, and stepping to the door, he looked in and then closed the door. Younger was in the middle of the street and seemed to be tightening his saddle girth.

"At the time J.S. Allen, the hardware dealer, came along and went toward the bank door, when Miller seized him roughly by the shoulders and, swearing furiously at him, and threatening him with a revolver, ordered him to stand back and keep quiet.

"Then I understood what was being done, and stepping off the sidewalk and into the street, I shouted, 'They're robbing the bank!" Younger and Miler turned to me and firing their revolvers over my head, shouted: 'Get in or we'll kill you!'"[197]

"I knew the bank was being robbed," Wheeler later recalled. "I knew how to handle a rifle. I had done a considerable amount of hunting, from fourteen on. But my rifle was at home, blocks away. I remembered suddenly that there was an army rifle and a sack of cartridges behind the desk at the Dampier House. I figured if I could get my hands on it that I could run upstairs to one of the front rooms of the hotel and start shooting from the window."[198]

According to Dr. Wheeler: "I was entirely unarmed and began to think it was time I was out of there, so I started for the drugstore for my gun, and as I ran, I saw three more men riding up the street, cursing and shooting right and left."[199]

Cole Younger and Clell Miller sprang into their saddles and shouted at Wheeler to get back. One of them shot at him as he ran to the drugstore for a gun. Unable to find one, Wheeler left by the back door and ran up the alley to the Dampier Hotel on the corner. "Dr. Dampier was behind the desk, and hurriedly explaining what I wanted, I took down the gun while he hunted for ammunition, but he could find only three cartridges," recalled Dr. Wheeler. Rushing through the lobby, he took up a position in a second-floor window.

The rifle was a .52 caliber Smith carbine, an early breech loading, single-shot relic from the Civil War. It used a separate foil-and-paper cartridge and a percussion cap.[200] "The street was a scene of confusion," said Wheeler, "as the five robbers were shooting in every direction and several of the residents were preparing to take a hand in the fray."[201]

JOHN KOBLAS

Dr. Wheeler, who had been one of the first to sound the alarm, had positioned himself in a second-story window when the fight began. Dr. Wheeler had taken a shot at Jim Younger, who had raced by, but his aim was high, and the bullet missed the outlaw. Jim looked around to see who nearly hit him, but by then, Dr. Wheeler's attention had shifted to another scene. After Elias Stacy blasted Clell Miller in the face with a load of birdshot, the outlaw quickly jumped back on his horse, but Dr. Wheeler shot him from the second-story window. The bullet severed the subclavian artery and killed him.

"When I stepped out of the drug store, a bullet whizzed by so close it drove me back," remembered Dr. Wheeler. "I made it the next time. I snatched up the rifle and cartridges behind the desk and raced upstairs. Across the street a man on horseback saw me and snapped a shot at me. He was using a pistol. I took dead aim on him, and he tumbled out of the saddle. I had killed him."[202]

Wheeler's third cartridge had fallen to the floor; useless because the paper out of which it was made was broken. But Dampier, the hotel owner, came to his rescue with fresh ammunition. This time he hit Bob Younger in the right elbow as he rushed from the bank.[203]

While a posse was forming to chase down the fleeing live bandits, Henry Wheeler, aware of the scarcity of cadavers at medical school, had an idea. There were more corpses lying in Northfield than the University of Michigan's dissection laboratory would see in a semester, and having killed one of the bad men, that one, he must have reasoned, belonged to him. Prisons, charity wards, and poor farms would often be given corpses but medical students in rural communities seldom were given the opportunity.[204]

Wheeler, Persons, and Dampier volunteered for burial detail, and the two dead outlaws were quickly buried in a potter's field in the southwest corner of the Northfield cemetery. This part of the graveyard was used for the burials of paupers and derelicts.

But Wheeler and his two cohorts returned to the graveyard that night and had no trouble finding the shallow and carefully marked graves. A nervous black wagon driver accompanied them, and the bodies of Chadwell and Miller were hastily dug up, nailed inside two barrels marked "paint" and driven out of town. The bodies were placed on a train in Minneapolis/St. Paul, which was bound for Michigan.[205]

Another account reported that Wheeler did join the posse, but in leaving Northfield, yelled to his friend, Persons, "Clarence, see if you can get the bodies." Clarence Persons stayed up all night preparing the bodies for the curious barrel shipment.[206]

Still another report alleged that the future Dr. Dampier "retrieved" the outlaw corpses from the graveyard while Wheeler was out with the posse. Initially, Mayor Solomon Stewart of Northfield had said the medical students could have the bodies, but later questioned his authority to give them up. But he did relate to the students that, while he had to bury the bandits, he did not think it necessary to bury them deeply. Of course, the young medical students took that as tacit permission to commit an act of good old-fashioned grave robbing.[207]

The three students soon returned to the University of Michigan campus with their two barrels of "paint." Their classmates looked upon them as heroes because the cadavers were in the prime of life and in excellent condition. When a friend asked Wheeler how he procured his cadaver, he answered proudly, "I shot him."[208]

Only a month following their return to school, the *Ann Arbor Courier* ran an account of their endeavors next to an advertisement for Ayers Sarsaparilla: "The students of the medical department will this winter have the pleasure of carving up two genuine robbers, being members of the Northfield, Minnesota, gang."[209]

Asked if he ever felt remorse for shooting the outlaw, Henry Wheeler answered: "Poppycock! The man got what he deserved! By serving as my cadaver he served a much higher purpose than he would have had he lived."[210]

Wheeler graduated in 1877 and entered practice in Northfield. Dr. Wheeler went to New York City where he entered the College of Physicians and Surgeons to obtain further training. He returned to Northfield from New York City to marry his high school sweetheart, Adeline Murray, on October 15, 1878. Less than three years later, Adeline died in childbirth. Both mother and infant were buried in Northfield's Oaklawn Cemetery.[211]

The obituary read: ". . . The infant daughter . . . after the brief stay of one day in the world, yielded up its life, and the day following . . . Mrs. Wheeler followed the little one. She was [twenty-eight] years old and six months. Her married life with Dr. Wheeler had been two years and eight months."[212]

In July 1881, Wheeler established a practice in Grand Forks, North Dakota, as a prominent surgeon. Dr. Wheeler brought one of the robber's skeletons with him when he started a medical practice in Grand Forks, North Dakota.

A Grand Forks patient of Dr. Wheeler, the mother of Erkle Longstreet of Northfield, said, during a visit at the office, that he produced a gun out of his desk drawer. He informed her that he always kept the gun handy because he was afraid of a visit from gang members that might wish to kill him. When she told him she was interested in the details of the Northfield raid, he pulled a string that opened a curtain and revealed the famous skeleton. The lady was astonished and shocked but was said to have kept her composure.[213]

But Dr. Wheeler dedicated much of his medical life to improvement of obstetrical procedures. In 1887, he was admitted to membership in the Dakota medical Society in Huron, South Dakota. He frequently refused payment for house calls and "occasionally would place a [ten-dollar] bill on the table as he left to hold the desperate family."[215]

He served as president of the North Dakota Medical Association in 1895-1896; Secretary of the Board of Medical Examiners from 1894 to 1911. He entered into partnership to form the Wheeler, Campbell, and Williamson Clinic in 1905. He served as city alderman and two years as mayor of Grand Forks. He was a Grand Master of the Masons, a member of the Modern Woodsmen, the Elks Club, and the Knights of Pythias.

During Wheeler's tenure as mayor, 1918 to 1920, he helped land the State Mill and Elevator, which greatly aided Grand Fork's development. Some people speculated that Grand Forks would become another major grain terminal such as Omaha.[215]

Dr. Wheeler was well respected in Grand Forks and was always a good sport, not minding when people poked fun. He was often a subject in the newspaper where reporters had fun with him as evidenced by the following article:

"Doctor Wheeler is in danger of losing his reputation as a marksman and received many condolences yesterday over his poor aim. It was like this; a partridge looked down upon the doctor from the top of a telephone pole at the Union National Bank corner. The doctor gazed at the stray visitor and brought forth a howitzer from the depths of his hip pocket and blazed away. The bird looked at him with a surprised expression, and the doctor fired another volley. The bird again looked surprised and took wing and sailed away."[216]

Dr. Wheeler married his second wife, Josephine E. Connell, a St. Cloud schoolteacher in 1884, and they constructed a beautiful house, modeled after that of his good friend, Empire Builder—James J. Hill. The home, located at 419 South Fifth Street, was built in 1885 and designed by John W. Ross, Grand Forks' leading architect at the time. The house was described as "the best example of a brick Italianate house dating from the mid-1880s on the North Dakota side of the Red River of the North."[217]

In a 1996 interview, Henry M. Wheeler jokingly said of Josephine, "She was spending the old boy's money; I'll tell you that."[218]

Wheeler's friendship with Hill must have been quite significant, as a 1927 article in the *Northfield News* implies, "The history of the Great Northern Railway could not be written and the name of Dr. H.M. Wheeler left out."[219] Because Hill and Wheeler were both sportsman, they cultivated a friendship that lasted for years. They hunted geese and deer together in North Dakota and northern Minnesota and sometimes prairie chickens in Nelson County. Widely acclaimed for his skill with firearms, Dr. Wheeler helped build a trapshooting club in Grand Forks and summer competitions were held at a local range twice a week.[220]

Josephine Wheeler passed away on August 24, 1914. Her obituary in the *Northfield News* read:

"Mrs. H.M. Wheeler, second wife of Dr. H.M. Wheeler of Grand Forks, [North Dakota], passed away in that city Monday evening according to a message received on Tuesday by Chas. Crary, a cousin of the doctor. The remains were brought here [Northfield] yesterday for interment in Oaklawn Cemetery.

"Dr. Wheeler was a resident of Northfield at the time of the Younger raid and took a prominent part in the fight on the robbers, firing the shot that proved fatal to one of the bandits."[221]

He married Ontario-born Mae M. McCulloch, in Grand Forks on July 3, 1922. Henry and Mae visited Northfield five months later as guests of Henry's sister-in-law Hattie Murray for two days. Henry was given a hometown welcome, and the newspaper assured its readers that "Manning and Wheeler were the ones who finally put the robbers to flight." According to the newspaper, few of the Northfield old-timers were left, but Wheeler renewed acquaintances with some of those who were still in the city.[222]

A son, Henry, was born to the Wheelers on April 20, 1925, when the doctor was nearly seventy-two years old.[223]

Wheeler was considered quite a character in Grand Forks. He won the first organized car race in Grand Forks with his steam-powered "locomobile," beating the runner-up, local dentist Dr.

Ramey's gas-powered entry by twenty-four inches. The local newspaper reported, "Dr. Ramsey doesn't believe in being in too much of a hurry whether pulling a tooth or the lever of his new auto."[224]

The man who had shot Clell Miller continued as a sharpshooter, moving his son, Henry Wheeler, Jr., to say, "Mom said he would fill the backseat of a Cadillac before breakfast."[225]

He was also quite an inventor, introducing a device for reharnessing horses in seconds rather than minutes. In 1887, he built the snow yacht, which allowed him to skim across the wintry Dakota prairies and placed him on the cover of Scientific American and in the pages of *Frank Leslie's Illustrated Weekly*. A reporter for the *Grand Forks Herald* described the snow yacht:

"It has two principal runners about [fifty]-feet long and eight-inches broad, with a third runner used as a rudder. The mast is about [twenty]-feet high with two sails attached of equal proportion." Wheeler's design made him the talk of the town.[226]

Over the first few days of April 1930, the Wheelers visited Northfield again, as they did several times over the years. Henry's sister-in-law, Hattie Murray, was seriously ill at her home on College Avenue. The Wheelers returned to Grand Forks after the visit.

Dr. Wheeler died of heart disease at 12:30 A.M., April 13, 1930, at the age of seventy-six, in his home. The *Northfield News* carried a lengthy obituary. Grand Forks City offices were closed as hundreds of people paid tribute in the Masonic Temple. The body was brought to Northfield following the service, and the local Masonic lodge conducted similar rites, with G.E. Raymond as master, and Dr. Samuel Johnson as chaplain. He was buried in the family lot at Oaklawn Cemetery.[227]

For many years his son owned the famous carbine his father had used in Northfield to thwart the outlaws but later sold the weapon. In appreciation of his bravery and assistance with defending the bank, Henry M. Wheeler was given a pocket watch by the First National Bank of Northfield. The inscription reads:

"H.M. Wheeler, From the First National Bank of Northfield, September 7, 1876." The watch was later donated to the Northfield Historical Society by his son, Henry Wheeler, Jr.[228]

Mrs. Mae Wheeler, husband of Henry, Sr., survived him by many years, passing away on March 22, 1967. Her body was brought to Northfield for interment in Oaklawn Cemetery.[229]

Frank J. Wilcox

FRANK J. WILCOX, THE SON OF BAPTIST MINISTER James F. Wilcox, was born in Taunton, Massachusetts, September 8, 1848. His father, born in Westminster, Vermont, in September 1806 had lived on a farm

until he was fifteen years old. At the age of eighteen, he taught school in Mason Village, New Hampshire. After teaching as well in New York and Massachusetts, he graduated from the Theological Seminary in Newton and was ordained a pastor of the Baptist church. After marrying Louisa Smith, the Wilcoxes had two children—Maria L., who died in 1866, and Frank J.[230]

At the age of five, Frank moved with his family to Trenton, New Jersey, and five years later to Northfield. He attended Carleton Preparatory School before getting a degree at the University of Chicago in 1874. According to W.F. Schilling, he was also treasurer of the State Fair for a number of years.[231] During the Northfield raid, he worked as an assistant at the First National Bank.

Frank J. Wilcox recalled that afternoon when he was suddenly startled by a noise at the door, only to look up and find three men with pistols in their hands: "I was in Northfield at two o'clock P.M., yesterday afternoon. [I] was in the bank when three men came into the bank. [I] was clerking in [the] bank at that time. [I] saw two men come to the bank counter and present revolvers. [They] ordered us to hold up our hands. Bunker and Heywood were also present at the time. Heywood [was] acting cashier. Bunker was also clerking at [the] bank at [the] time as teller. The three men sprang onto [the] counter and over. [They] said they were going to rob [the] bank and asked for [the] cashier. Then [they] ordered us on [our] knees with hands [up and] demanded of each of us whether we were the cashier. We each said we were not and then [they] demanded [that the] safe should be opened. [The] vault door being open, one went in. Mr. Heywood sprang to close [the] door on him and [the] other two dragged him back. In some way Heywood broke loose and rose. [He] called out, 'Murder!'"[232]

One of the robbers screamed, "We've got forty men outside."[233] Wilcox believed that the outlaws did not see Heywood when they came in, as he was sitting off to the side at a desk with a high front, which partially concealed him. When they demanded the cashier open the vault, Heywood jumped up and was promptly ordered to his knees with his hands up. According to Wilcox, the three outlaws were Bob Younger, Charlie Pitts, and probably Frank James. Wilcox was sure the men had been drinking because the smell of liquor was very strong.

Wilcox was given a permanent position following the robbery. When Alonzo Bunker left the bank, Mr. Wilcox stepped up to his position as assistant cashier. In 1879, he married Jennie M. Blake. Wilcox and his wife later followed their sons, James and Hugh, to Yakima, Washington.

"In my ramblings I happened in that town just ten days before he died," wrote W.F. Schilling. "He and Mrs. Wilcox took me over to see the beautiful new mausoleum being erected, and as we left it to go to the train, he said, "William, the next time you come this way I, in all probability, will be in here," pointing to one of the two crypts he had purchased for himself and Mrs. Wilcox. I had not been at home ten days when one evening I received a wire stating that my good friend was one of the first to enter the new structure."[234]

Frank Wilcox passed away December 23, 1921 in Yakima, Washington.[235]

Notes

[1] "Minnesotans' Account of the Raid," *The Northfield Magazine*, Volume 6, Number 2, 1992, pp. 9-10.
[2] *Northfield News*, July 10, 1897.
[3] *Rice County Journal*, November 16, 1889.
[4] Reverend Edward Neill, *History of Rice County Including Explorers and Pioneers of Minnesota and Outline History of the State of Minnesota*, Minneapolis, Minnesota Historical Society, 1882, p. 424.
[5] Blanche Butler Ames, *Chronicles from the Nineteenth Century Family Letters of Blanche Butler & Adelbert Ames*, Volume I, pp. I, xi.
[6] James Grant Wilson and John Fiske, editors, *Appleton's Cyclopedia of American Biography*, six volumes, New York: D. Appleton and Company, 1887-1889 & edited Stanley L. Klos, 1999 reprint; *American National Biography; Dictionaryof American Biography*; Ames, Blanche, *Adelbert Ames, 1835-1933, General Senator, Governor*, North Easton, Massachusetts: Argosy Antiquarian, 1964; Kirshner, Ralph, *The Class of 1861: Custer, Ames, and Their Classmates after West Point*, Carbondale: Southern Illinois University Press, 1999.
[7] Ted P. Yeatman, *Frank and Jesse James*, p. 170.
[8] Stuart B. Lord, "Adelbert Ames Soldier & Politician a Reevaluation," *Maine Historical Society Quarterly*, Volume 13, Number 2, Fall 1973, pp. 87-88; Pejepscot Historical Society letter to author dated February 3, 2001.
[9] Samuel J. Martin, *Southern Hero Matthew Galbraith Butler*, Mechanicsburg, Pennsylvania, Stackpole Books, 2001, pp. 169-170.
[10] Ibid.
[11] Stuart B. Lord, "Adelbert Ames Soldier & Politician a Reevaluation," *Maine Historical Society Quarterly*, Fall 1973, pp. 87-88.

¹²Ibid.
¹³Blanche Butler Ames, *Chronicles from the Nineteenth Century Family Letters of Blanche Butler & Adelbert Ames*, Volume 1, 1861-1874, privately issued, 1957, p. 1,38.
¹⁴Stuart B. Lord, "Adelbert Ames Soldier & Politician A Reevaluation," *Maine Historical Society Quarterly*, Fall 1973, pp. 89-90.
¹⁵Bob Warn, "Nuggets from Rice County, Southern Minnesota History," *Golden Nugget*, pp. 11-14.
¹⁶Ibid.; *Northfield, Minnesota Centennial 1855 Century of Progress 1955*, p. 27.
¹⁷Ibid.
¹⁸Blanche Butler Ames, *Chronicles from the Nineteenth Century Family Letters of Blanche Butler & Adelbert Ames*, Volume 1, 1861-1874, p. 289.
¹⁹Ibid., p. 308.
²⁰Bob Warn, "Historical Bank Raid Centered on Ames Family," in "Nuggets from Rice County, Southern Minnesota History," *Golden Nugget*, May 17, 1972, p. ll; *Time-Life Books*, p. 145; Ted P. Yeatman, *Frank and Jesse James*, pp. 171-171.
²¹*New York Times*, January 29, 1874.
²²Stuart B. Lord, "Adelbert Ames Soldier & Politician A Reevaluation," *Maine Historical Society Quarterly*, Fall 1973, pp. 91-92.
²³Samuel J. Martin, *Southern Hero Matthew Galbraith Butler*, pp. 204-205.
²⁴Blanche Butler Ames, *Chronicles from the Nineteenth Century Family Letters of Blanche Butler & Adelbert Ames*, Volume 1, 1861-1874, p. 698.
²⁵Ibid., p. 707; Ibid., Volume 2, pp. 286-287.
²⁶Blanche Ames Ames, *Broken Oaths and Reconstruction in Mississippi, 1835-1933*, New York, Argosy-Antiquarian Ltd., 1964, p. 453.
²⁷*The Testimony in the Impeachment of Adelbert Ames as Governor of Mississippi*, Jackson, Mississippi, Power & Barksdale, State Printers, 1877, pp. 22-48.
²⁸Blanche Butler Ames, *Chronicles from the Nineteenth Century Family Letters of Blanche Butler & Adelbert Ames*, Volume 2, pp. 304-305.
²⁹Ibid., p. 346.
³⁰Ibid., pp. 352-353.
³¹Blanche Ames Ames, *Broken Oaths and Reconstruction in Mississippi, 1835-1933*, pp. 469-471.
³²*New York Times*, May 2, 1876.
³³Blanche Ames Ames, *Broken Oaths and Reconstruction in Mississippi, 1835-1933*, p. 471.
³⁴Bob Warn, *Golden Nugget*.
³⁵*Northfield News*, December 6, 1894; General Ledger First National Bank of Northfield; *Northfield, Minnesota, Centennial 1855 Century of Progress 1955*, p. 27.
³⁶Ibid.
³⁷Marley Brant, *The Outlaw Youngers: A Confederate Brotherhood*; Lanham, New York & London, Madison Books, 1992, p. 175.

[38] Ted P. Yeatman, *Frank and Jesse James*, p. 172.
[39] *Honey Grove Signal*, April 2, 1915.
[40] Blanche Butler Ames, *Chronicles from the Nineteenth Century Family Letters of Blanche Butler & Adelbert Ames*, Volume 2, p. 402.
[41] W. F. Schilling, *Up and Down Main Street 40 years Ago, Reminiscences of Northfield*; Northfield, *Northfield News*, 1935, p. 19.
[42] Bob Warn, *Golden Nugget*, pp. 11-14.
[43] Blanche Butler Ames, *Chronicles from the Nineteenth Century Family Letters of Blanche Butler & Adelbert Ames*, Volume 2, p. 404.
[44] Blanche Butler Ames, *Chronicles from the Nineteentr Century Family Letters of Blanche Butler & Adelbert Ames*, Volume 2, p. 403.
[45] Blanche Ames Ames, *Adelbert Ames Broken Oaths and Reconstruction in Mississippi, 1835-1933*, New York, Argosy-Antiquarian Ltd., 1964, pp. 495, 500.
[46] Bob Warn, *Golden Nugget*, p. 11.
[47] *Martin County* (Fairmont) *Sentinel*, October 6, 1876.
[48] Blanche Butler Ames, *Chronicles from the Nineteenth Century Family Letters of Blanche Butler & Adelbert Ames*, Volume 2, p. 405.
[49] Maggie Lee, editor, "Defeat Unfolds," *Defeat of the Jesse James Gang*, August 1981, p. 14.
[50] Blanche Butler Ames, *Chronicles from the Nineteenth Century Family Letters of Blanche Butler & Adelbert Ames*, Volume 2, pp. 408-409.
[51] Ibid.
[52] Reverend Edward Neill, *History of Rice County Including Explorers and Pioneers of Minnesota and Outline History of the State of Minnesota*, Minneapolis, Minnesota Historical Society, 1882, p. 405; *Rice County Families: Their History Our Heritage*, Faribault, Rice County Historical Society, 1981, pp. 383-400.
[53] Stuart B. Lord, "Adelbert Ames Soldier & Politician: A Reevaluation," *Maine Historical Society Quarterly*, Fall 1973, p. 94.
[54] *Northfield News*, August 3, 1929; Bob Warn, *Golden Nugget*.
[55] *New York Times*, April 26, 1933.
[56] *Those Who Answered the Call: A Scrapbook of Information about the Madelia Posse and the Younger Brothers Gang*, The Bradford Story, Mankato, Watonwan Historical Society, 1999, no page numbers.
[57] George A. Bradford letter to D.E. Hasey, January 20, 1924. Copy in author's collection.
[58] *Mankato Weekly Review*, Tuesday, September 26, 1876.
[59] George A. Bradford letter to D.E. Hasey, January 20, 1924.
[60] *Those Who Answered the Call*; George Huntington, *Robber and Hero*, pp. 96-97.
[61] *St. Paul Dispatch*, Sunday, September 10, 1876, p. 1.
[62] Chris Roberts, "The Northfield Raid in Verse," *NOLA Quarterly*, October-December 1998; *Mankato Weekly Review*, September 12, 1876.
[63] *Faribault Republican*, September 13, 1876, p. 3.
[64] *St. Paul Dispatch*, Sunday, September 10,1876, p.1.

[65] Blue Earth County Sheriff Peter Schweitzer affidavit dated July 12, 1880. District Court, Blue Earth County Courthouse, Mankato, Minnesota.
[66] *Mankato Weekly Review*, July 20, 1880.
[67] Ibid. The revolver was found on Pitts' body following the robbery attempt and taken by an identified person as a souvenir.
[68] Ibid.
[69] George Huntington, *Robber and Hero*, pp. 85-87.
[70] *Mankato Weekly Review*, Tuesday, September 26, 1876.
[71] *The Northfield Saga*, p. 11.
[72] *Mankato Weekly Review*, Tuesday, September 26, 1876.
[73] *Mankato Weekly Review*, September 26, 1876.
[74] *Mankato Free Press*, Wednesday, September 19, 1979.
[75] *Mankato Weekly Review*, September 26, 1876.
[76] *Mankato Weekly Review*, Tuesday, September 12, 1876.
[77] *Mankato Free Press*, September 20, 1979, John Stone, "Shoot-out on the Watonwan, The Younger Gang Comes to Madelia," p. 6C-7C.
[78] *Plat Book of Watonwan County, Minnesota*, Philadelphia, Interstate Publishing Company, 1886, pp. 20-21.
[79] Rex Macbeth, *The Minnesota Magnificent Seven*.
[80] *Mankato Free Press*, September 20, 1979.
[81] *Mankato Free Press*, September 20, 1979.
[82] Owen R. Dickie letter to LeSueur County Historical Society dated January 30, 1971.
[83] Cole Younger, *The Story of Cole Younger by Himself*, p. 86.
[84] *Mankato Weekly Review*, August 10, 1880.
[85] "Funeral Discourse of Joseph Lee Heywood," September 10, 1876. General Ledger First National Bank of North field; Sharon Gates-Hull, "Not Just Cowboys Women-Wives, Daughters-Played Roles in the Saga of Jesse James," *Northfield News*, Souvenir Edition, Friday, September 11, 1998.
[86] *St. Paul & Minneapolis Pioneer Press and Tribune*, Saturday, September 9, 1876, "The Dead Cashier," p. 2; The Northfield Bank Raid, p. 4; Sue Garwood-DeLong interview with author March 19, 2001.
[87] George Huntington, *Robber and Hero*, p. 17.
[88] George Huntington, *Robber and Hero*, pp. 18-19.
[89] *Northfield News*, Saturday, July 10, 1897.
[90] *The Madelia Times*, November 20, 1896, A.E. Bunker, "Recollections of the Northfield Raid," p. 6.
[91] Ibid; *Minneapolis Tribune*, Sunday, April 4, 1982, "A Century after His Death, Jesse James Still Good Copy" by Mark Peterson, p. 13A.
[92] *Minneapolis Tribune*, Friday Evening, September 8, 1876, "Northfield's Sensation," p. 1.
[93] *Northfield News*, Saturday, July 10, 1897.
[94] *St. Paul Pioneer Press & Tribune*, Friday, September 8, 1876.
[95] Sharon Gates-Hull, "Not Just Cowboys Women-Wives, Daughters-Played Roles in the Saga of Jesse James, *Northfield News*, Souvenir Edition,

Friday, September 11, 1998, p. 5; George Huntington, *Robber and Hero*, pp. 39-40.

[96] *St. Paul Sunday Pioneer Press*, August 28, 1966.

[97] Reverend Delavan L. Leonard, D.D., *The History of Carleton College: Its Origin and Growth, Environment and Builders*, Chicago, Fleming H. Revell Company, 1904, pp. 150-151.

[98] Sharon Gates-Hull, "Not Just Cowboys Women-Wives, Daughters-Played Roles in the Saga of Jesse James," *Northfield News*, Souvenir Edition, Friday, September 11, 1998, p. 5.

[99] Ibid.

[100] Ibid.

[101] *Northfield News*, June 15, 1901.

[102] *Northfield News*, Saturday, July 10, 1897.

[103] Ibid.

[104] *Northfield News*, March 7, 1896.

[105] *NorthfieldNews*, June 15, 1901.

[106] *Northfield News*, June 22, 1901.

[107] Augustine E. Costello, *History of the Fire and Police Departments of Minneapolis: Their Origin, Progress, and Development*.

[108] *The Klondike Weekly*, Dawson City, Yukon Territory, May 1, 1998.

[109] Augustine E. Costello, *History of the Fire and Police Departments of Minneapolis: Their Origin, Progress, and Development*.

[110] William Watts Folwell, *History of Minnesota*, Volume III, Appendix 5, St. Paul: Minnesota Historical Society, 1969, pp. 372-374; Marion D. Shutter, *History of Minneapolis: Gateway to the Northwest*, Vol. II, Minneapolis: S.J. Clarke Publishing Company, 1923, pp. 787-788; *New York Sun*, January 3, 1893; *St. Paul Pioneer Press*, July 31, 1873; *Minneapolis Tribune*, July 17, 1873; (Winnipeg) *Manitoba Free Press*, July 12, 1873.

[111] *St. Paul Pioneer Press*, July 31, 1873.

[112] William Watts Folwell, *History of Minnesota*, Volume III, pp. 374-376.

[113] Ibid., p. 374.

[114] *Minneapolis Tribune*, July 18, 1873; *Manitoba Free Press*, July 12 and 19, 1873.

[115] *Minneapolis Journal*, October 1, 1905.

[116] William Watts Folwell, *History of Minnesota*, Volume III, pp. 384-388.

[117] Chris Roberts, "The Northfield Raid in Verse," *NOLA Quarterly*, October-December 1998, p.13.

[118] *Minneapolis Tribune*, September 9, 1876.

[119] *Mankato Free Press*, Monday, April 5, 1937, "Youngers Led Raid on Bank," *Madelia Times-Messenger*, Thursday, July 4, 1957, "Capture of Younger Brothers."

[120] *Mankato Weekly Review*, September 26, 1876.

[121] Chris Roberts, "The Northfield Raid in Verse," *NOLA Quarterly*, October-December 1998, p.13.

[122] Ibid.
[123] Ibid.
[124] *Mankato Record*, Saturday, September 23, 1876.
[125] *Minneapolis Tribune*, September 17, 1876.
[126] *Minneapolis Tribune*, September 15, 1876.
[127] *Faribault Republican*, September 20, 1876, "Blunder of Hoy," p.3.
[128] Obituary Files, Northfield Public Library; Bob Phelps, "Remember the Name Manning—'the Man for the Emergency,'" *Northfield News*, Friday, September 5, 1997, p. 7; Robert Phelps interview with author March 19, 2001, Northfield.
[129] Bob Phelps, "Remember the Name Manning—'the Man for the Emergency,'" *Northfield News*, Friday, September 5, 1997, pp. 6-7.
[130] *NorthfieldNews*, Saturday, July 10, 1897.
[131] *Martin County Sentinel*, September 8, 1876.
[132] *Northfield News*, Saturday, July 10, 1876.
[133] Bob Phelps, "Remember the Name Manning—'the Man for the Emergency,'" *Northfield News*, Friday, September 5, 1997.
[134] *Northfield News*, Saturday, July 10, 1876.
[135] Ibid.
[136] Ibid.; Bob Phelps, "Remember the Name Manning—'the Man for the Emergency,'" *Northfield News*, Friday, September 5, 1997.
[137] *Minneapolis Tribune*, Friday Evening, September 8, 1876.
[138] George Huntington, *Robber and Hero*, pp. 32.
[139] Bob Phelps, "Remember the Name Manning—'the Man for the Emergency,'" *Northfield News*, Friday, September 5, 1997.
[140] *Madelia Times-Messenger*, August 27, 1904.
[141] Franklin L. Sorenson, "Story of Part Which Norwegian Lad Took in Capturing the Notorious Younger Gang," Rex Macbeth, *The Minnesota Magnificent Seven*.
[142] Rex Macbeth, *The Minnesota Magnificent Seven*.
[143] *Northfield News*, Saturday, July 10, 1897. Account of T. L. Vought.
[144] *New Ulm Journal*, January 12, 1939, "Old-Timers Remember Younger Gang; Captured Near Here After Robbery."
[145] *Madelia Times-Messenger*, August 27, 1904.
[146] *Mankato Record*, August 17, 1878.
[147] *Mankato Record*, August 24, 1878.
[148] Ibid.
[149] *Mankato Record*, January 4, 1879.
[150] *Mankato Record*, February 8, 1879.
[151] *Mankato Record*, March 8, 1879.
[152] *Mankato Free Press*, November 14, 1879.
[153] *Madelia Times-Messenger*, August 27, 1904.
[154] *Final Report on the Battlefield of Gettysburg (New York at Gettysburg)* by the New York Monuments Commission for the Battlefields of Gettysburg and Chattanooga. Albany, NY: J.B. Lyon Company, 1902.

[155] Frederick Phisterer, *New York in the War of the Rebellion*, 3rd edition, Albany: J.B. Lyon Company, 1912.
[156] *Mankato Review*, December 8, 1885, and April 15, 1884.
[157] *Mankato Free Press*, Obituary, June 15, 1906.
[158] Ibid.
[159] *Mankato Review*, December 8, 1885; *Mankato Review*, April 15, 1884; *Mankato Free Press*, June 15, 1906.
[160] A.O. Sorbel letter to Carl Weicht dated August 19, 1929. Author's collection.
[161] *St. James Plain Dealer*, October 16, 1924, "Sorbel of Webster, Ia. (sic-S.D.), Tells of His Work in Capture of Youngers," p.4; *Sioux Falls* (S.D.) *Argus-Leader*, series of articles by J.A. Derome March 22-June 4, 1924, "Webster Man Gives His Story of James-Younger Raid; Was First to tell of Gang's Hiding Place."
[162] A.O. Sorbel letter to Carl Weicht.
[163] *Mankato Weekly Review*, September 26, 1876.
[164] *St. James Plain Dealer*, October 16, 1924; *Sioux Falls Argus Leader*.
[165] *Hanska Herald*; Friday, March 18, 1949, "Hanska Community Centennial Memorial," papers of Inga Sorbel, p. 1; *Mankato Free Press*, Thursday, May 20, 1993, As told by Nettie (Sorbel) Asleson, pp. 13, 15.
[166] Chuck Parsons, "Madelia's Paul Revere—Nemesis of the Younger Gang," *The English Westerners Tally Sheet*, April 1977, Vol. 23, No. 3, p. 2.
[167] *Mankato Weekly Review*, September 26, 1876.
[168] A.O. Sorbel letter to Carl Weicht.
[169] *St. James Plain Dealer*, October 16, 1924.
[170] *Mankato Weekly Review*, September 26, 1876.
[171] Rex Macbeth, *The Minnesota Magnificent Seven*, 1996.
[172] "Captured at Madelia," Source unknown, Author's Collection.
[173] *Mankato Weekly Review*, September 26, 1876.
[174] Buster Yates, *Seventy-Five Years on the Watonwan*, Madelia, December 1986, p. 159.
[175] *Mankato Weekly Review*, September 26, 1876.
[176] "Captured at Madelia."
[177] *Mankato Weekly Review*, September 26, 1876.
[178] A.O. Sorbel letter to Carl Weicht.
[179] *St. James Plain Dealer*, October 16, 1924.
[180] *St. James Plain Dealer*, October 16, 1924.
[181] Ibid.
[182] *Minneapolis Tribune*, September 23, 1876.
[183] *Mankato Record*, February 8, 1879.
[184] A.R. Sorbel letter to Chuck Parsons dated August 23, 1976.
[185] *Reporter and Farmer* (Webster, S.D.), July 17, 1930.
[186] *The Northfield Saga*, p. 9; In *Madelia Times*, November 20, 1896, a clerk, Joseph B. Hyde was given credit as being the birdshot marksman.
[187] *Canadian Gleaner* (Huntington, Quebec), October 18, 1877; *Rice County Journal*, November 1, 1877.

[188] *Northfield News*, March 23, 1882.
[189] Franklin L. Sorenson, "Story of Part Which Norwegian Lad Took In Capturing the Notorious Younger Bros.," Undated *Blue Earth Post* article, Watonwan Historical Society, Made1ia.
[190] *Northfield News*, July 25, 1930, Oscar Sorbel Obituary.
[191] *Webster* (S.D.) *Journal*, July 17, 1930, T.L. Vought, "As Boy and Man."
[192] Woodrow Keljik, "The 1st . . . Last of a Long Line," *Ace* magazine of the St. Paul Athletic Club, May 1984, Vol. 64, No.5, p. 6; Christine Taylor Thompson, Cottonwood County Historical Society, Windom, letters to author dated January 6, 1997, and January 16, 1997; Jay Donald, *Outlaws of the Border: A Complete and Authentic History of Frank and Jesse James, The Younger Brothers,* The Coburn & Newman Publishing Company, Chicago, 1882, p. 304.
[193] *Mankato Free Press*, September 20, 1979.
[194] *Northfield News*, Saturday, July 10, 1897, Account of T.L. Vought.
[195] Orrin Delong, unpublished manuscript; Orrin Delong interview with author March 19, 2001, Northfield; Sue Garwood-Delong, "Dr. Wheeler," From Northfield Historical Society Exhibit "The Stories Behind the Story," 1996; Sue Garwood Delong interview with author March 19, 2001; Annalee Larson, "Hero of the Famous Raid, Henry Wheeler, a Renaissance Man in the Rest of His Life," *Northfield News*, Souvenir Edition, Friday, September 11, 1998, p. 4.
[196] *The Northfield Saga*, p.6; Lester E. Swanberg, *Then and Now: A History of Rice County*, under "Bank Is Raided," pp. 181-182; *Faribault Democrat*, September 15, 1876.
[197] Dr. Keith W. Millette Collection.
[198] George Turner, *Secrets of Jesse James*, Amarillo, Baxter Lane Co., 1975, p. 29.
[199] Dr. Keith W. Millette Collection.
[200] Ted P. Yeatman, *Frank and Jesse James*, p. 174.
[201] Dr. Keith W. Millette Collection.
[202] George Turner, *Secrets of Jesse James*, p. 29.
[203] Carl W. Breihan, *Younger Brothers,* The Naylor Company, San Antonio, 1961, pp. .178-179; *Mankato Free Press*, Wednesday, September 19, 1979, "Northfield Robbers Left State in an Uproar" by John Stone, p. 12.
[204] Sue Garwood Delong, Executive Director Northfield Historical Society interview with author, January 27, 1997, Northfield, Minnesota; Charles N. Barnard, Editor, *A Treasury of True: The Best From Twenty Years of the Man's Magazine,* A.S. Barnes and Company, New York, 1956, "You Shot Him—He's Yours," by William Bender, Jr., p. 239; Francis F. McKinney, "The Northfield Raid, and Its Ann Arbor Sequel," *Michigan Alumnus Quarterly Review 61*, December 4, 1954, pp. 38-45; William Holtz, "Bankrobbers, Burkers, and Bodysnatchers," *Michigan Quarterly Review*, 6, Spring 1967, pp. 90-98; *St. Paul Pioneer Press*, September 5, 1981, under "Others Reap Northfield Raid Riches" by Roger Barr; Clell Miller and William Stiles Files, Northfield Historical Society.

[205] Ibid.; Annalee Larson, "Hero of the Famous Raid, Henry Wheeler, a Renaissance Man in the Rest of His Life," *Northfield News*, Souvenir Edition, Friday, September 11, 1998, p. 4.

[206] *Rochester Post Bulletin*, Saturday, May 8, 1982, Ken McCracken, "Medical Research Got Help from James Gang."

[207] *Grand Forks Herald*, Date Unknown, Jack Hagerty, "Skeleton Had a Life of its Own," in collection of Keith W. Millette, M.D.

[208] *Rochester Post Bulletin*, Saturday, May 8, 1982, Ken McCracken, "Medical Research Got Help from James Gang."

[209] William Bender, Jr., "You Shot Him—He's Yours," p. 239.

[210] Annalee Larson, "Hero of the Famous Raid, Henry Wheeler, a Renaissance Man in the Rest of His Life," *Northfield News*, Souvenir Edition, Friday, September 11, 1998, p. 4; Bert Schiller, "Get Your Guns Boys, They're Robbing the Bank," *Michigan Today*, Summer 2002.

[211] Orrin DeLong, unpublished manuscript; Orrin DeLong interview with author March 19, 2001, Northfield; Sue Garwood-DeLong, "Dr. Wheeler," From Northfield Historical Society Exhibit "The Stories Behind the Story," 1996; Sue Garwood DeLong interview with author March 19, 2001; Annalee Larson, "Hero of the Famous Raid, Henry Wheeler, a Renaissance Man in the Rest of His Life," *Northfield News*, Souvenir Edition, Friday, September 11, 1998, p. 4.

[212] *Rice County Journal*, June 28, 1881.

[213] "Skeleton Burned Wheeler Questions Answered," *Northfield News*, December 7, 1979.

[214] Sue Garwood DeLong, "Dr. Wheeler," from Northfield Historical Society Exhibit, "The Stories Behind the Story," 1996.

[215] Steven B. Grosz and Steven R. Hoftbeck, "Unforgettable North Dakotans," *Horizons*, undated article in collection of Orrin DeLong.

[216] *Grand Forks Herald*; October 23, 1897.

[217] Steven B. Grosz and Steven R. Hoftbeck, "Unforgettable North Dakotans," *Horizons*, undated article in collection of Orrin DeLong.

[218] Henry M. Wheeler, Jr. interview with Orrin DeLong April 1996, Hastings.

[219] *Northfield News*, Friday, July 15, 1927; "Greater Grand Forks: A Downtown Walking Tour," in collection of Orrin DeLong; Dr. D. Jerome Tweton and Everett C. Albers, "Who Was Henry M. Wheeler?" *Presenting Prairie People*, The North Dakota Humanities Council, a video series.

[220] Steven B. Grosz and Steven R. Hoffbeck, "Unforgettable North Dakotans," *Horizons*, undated article in collection of Orrin DeLong.

[221] *Northfield News*, August 28, 1914.

[222] *Northfield News*, Friday, December 15, 1922.

[223] *Northfield News*, Friday, May 9, 1924; Sue Garwood DeLong, "Dr. Wheeler," from Northfield Historical Society Exhibit, "The Stories Behind the Story," 1996; *Grand Forks* (N.D.) *Herald*; April 14, 1929; Dr. Bill Powers, "History of Valley Medical Associates, Ltd."

[224] Sue Garwood DeLong, "Dr. Wheeler."

[225] Bill Powers, "History of Valley Medical Association, Ltd."
[226] Steven B. Grosz and Steven R. Hoffbeck, "Unforgettable North Dakotans," *Horizons*, undated article in collection of Orrin DeLong.
[227] *Northfield News*, Friday, April 18, 1930.
[228] Sue Garwood DeLong, "Dr. Wheeler."
[229] *Northfield News*, March 30, 1967.
[230] Reverend Edward Neill, *History of Rice County Including Explorers and Pioneers of Minnesota and Outline History of the State of Minnesota*, p. 436.
[231] W.F. Schilling, *Up and Down Main Street 40 Years Ago 1895-1935*, Northfield, Northfield News, 1935, p. 12.
[232] "Minnesotans' Accounts of the Raid," *The Northfield Magazine*, Volume 6, Number 2, 1992, p. 10.
[233] *Northfield News*, Saturday, July 10, 1897.
[234] W. F. Schilling, *Up and Down Main Street 40 Years Ago 1895-1935*, p. 12.
[235] *Northfield News*, Saturday, July 10, 1897; Obituary Files, Northfield Public Library.